ENVIRONMENTAL POLICIES IN INDIA

ENVIRONMENTAL POLICIES IN INDIA

Abhay Kumar
Surjith Karthikeyan

GYAN

ISBN: 978-81-212-1275-5

Price: ₹ 520

First Published, 2015

Published by

Gyan Publishing House
23, Main Ansari Road
Daryaganj, New Delhi-110002
Phones: 23282060, 23261060
Fax : 91-11-23285914
E-mail: books@gyanbooks.com

Laser Typesetting: Gyaan Print, Delhi
Printed at: G. Print Process, Delhi

Cataloging in Publication Data—DK

Courtesy: D.K. Agencies (P) Ltd. <docinfo@dkagencies.com>

Kumar, Abhay, author.

Environmental policies in India / Abhay Kumar, Surjith Karthikeyan.

pages cm

ISBN 9788121212755

1. Environmental policy—India. 2. Sustainable development—India. 3. Environmental impact charges—India. I. Karthikeyan, Shri Surjith, author. II. Title.

DDC 363.705610954 23

Dedicated to

Our Parents and Teachers

Contents

Preface and Acknowledgements

The key environmental challenges in India have been sharper in the past two decades. The State of the Environment Report by the Ministry of Environment, Forest & Climate Change clubs the issues under five key challenges faced by India, which are climate change, food security, water security, energy security, and managing urbanization. Climate change is impacting the natural adverse effects in India, mainly on agriculture on which 58 per cent of the population still depends for livelihood, water storage in the Himalayan glaciers which are the source of major rivers and groundwater recharge, sea-level rise, and threats to a long coastline and habitations. Climate change will also cause increased frequency of extreme events such as floods, and droughts. These in turn will impact India's food security problems and water security. As per the Second National Communication submitted by India to the United Nations Framework Convention on Climate Change (UNFCCC), it is projected that the annual mean surface air temperature rise by the end of the century ranges from 3.5°C to 4.3°C whereas the sea level along the Indian coast has been rising at the rate of about 1.3 mm/year on an average. These climate change projections are likely to impact human health, agriculture, water resources, natural ecosystems, and biodiversity.

India has been part of 94 multilateral environmental agreements. India has also voluntarily agreed to reduce its emission intensity of its GDP by 20-25 per cent over 2005 levels by 2020, and emissions from the agriculture sector would not form part of the assessment of its emissions intensity. Indian economy is already moving along a lower carbon and sustainable path in terms of declining carbon intensity of its GDP which is expected to fall further through lower carbon strategies. It is estimated that India's per capita emission in

2031 will still be lower than the global per capita emission in 2005 (in 2031, India's per capita GHG emissions will be under 4 tonnes of carbon dioxide equivalent (CO_2eq.) which is lower than the global per capita emissions of 4.22 tonnes of CO_2eq. in 2005).

Together with efforts to incorporate sustainability in the rural development process, India is increasingly making efforts to integrate the three pillars of sustainable development into its national policy space. In fact, environment protection is enshrined in our Constitution (Articles 48 A and 51 A [g]). Various policy measures are being implemented across the domains of forestry, pollution control, water management, clean energy, and marine and coastal environment. Some of these are policies like Joint Forest Management, Green Rating for Integrated Habitat Assessment, Coastal Zone Regulation Zone, eco labeling and energy efficiency labeling, fuel efficiency standards etc.

Despite all these efforts, the reality that confronts us on the environmental front continues to be harsh and complex. Increasing population, urbanization, and growing demand for water and land resources have severely impacted the quality and availability of water and soil resources. Rising energy needs is another area of concern. Besides, rapid growth will require corresponding growth in energy supply. Presently a large share of our energy demand is met through coal and oil and this trend will continue, given the unprecedented surge in energy demand and resource constraints. Energy issues become more complex with existing energy poverty and rise in energy prices. There is considerable scope for increasing efficiency in the use of energy and water in India together with other development indicators like Infant Mortality Rate, Maternity Mortality Rate, sanitation facilities, and public health services. Economic instruments, regulatory measures, and market mechanisms can play an important role in helping to achieve development and growth in a sustainable manner.

Through this book, the authors are trying to review the policies adopted in India towards protection of environment and abatement of pollution and sites the importance of a judicious mix of incentives and fiats based regulatory instruments for environment regulation. The basic approaches to Environmental Policy in general adopted in various Countries gives an overview of the pros and cons of their experience in environmental regulation. The authors are trying to bring under one umbrella the green initiative legislations in India under the purview of several Ministries and other government bodies. Sustainability has become guiding principles to emerging recalcitrant environment problems such as climate change and ozone depletion. There has been growing realization that Market Based Instruments (MBIs) such as ecological tax (eco tax) are much better tool available to policy makers to regulate behaviour of individuals/firms towards environment.

The views expressed in this book are authors' personal views and in no way corresponds to the views of Government of India. This book is mainly an eye opener to the policy makers, as it contains some good initiatives adopted in Developed Countries. This book is quite useful for students of Environmental Economics in colleges and universities, candidates preparing for Civil Service Examination, Indian Economic Service Examination and other competitive examinations as it contains the latest initiatives of Government of India towards Sustainable Development & Climate Change.

The authors deem it great privilege and pleasure in presenting this book which is an outcome of the experience gained in this area through constant interactions, discussions with environmental experts, policy makers in various countries and colleagues in their Service. The authors are immensely grateful for them in this regard.

Introduction

India's higher economic growth during the last decade has provided employment opportunities to its citizen. However, India's faster growth has come at cost of degradation of environment and growing scarcity of natural resources. In January 2014, the Yale ranked India 155 out of 178 on overall Environmental Performance Index and 174th out of 178 countries on air pollution. Degraded environment can pose a serious constraint to sustainability of economic growth. According to a report by the World Bank, environmental degradation costs India \$80 billion per year or 5.7% of its economy. As population and urbanization grow and consumption pattern change, pressure on country's natural resources-air, water, land and forests-will gradually increase. For an environmentally sustainable future, India needs to value its natural resources, and ecosystem services to better inform policy and decision-making especially since India is a hotspot of unique biodiversity and ecosystems.

Environmental costs are significant costs for system of production and consumption of goods and services. It has long term inter-generational implications emanating from leaving for the future generations a highly polluted environment. It also has significant implications for the present generations in terms of health hazards and quality of life that pollution entails. Emissions of carbon dioxide and other so-called "greenhouse gases" (like methane, nitrous oxide, chlorofluorocarbons and related compounds, non-methane volatile organic compounds, and water vapour) are contributing to 'global climate change'.

Differences in pollution levels across countries or states within a country with large geographic areas as is the case in India depend, among other factors, on the level and structure of demand for goods and services, which may be produced by polluting inputs and processes. Effects of pollution are different for local, regional, national, and global perspectives. Depending on the nature of pollution and its effects, policies to abate pollution also need to be different.

Approaches to Environment Policy vary in different Countries. The first chapter of this book reviews the policies adopted in India towards protection of environment and abatement of pollution. The National Environment Policy (NEP), 2006 is such a policy intended to be a guide to action in regulatory reform, programmes and projects for environmental conservation; and review and enactment of legislation, by agencies of the Central, State, and Local Governments. The Principle of economic efficiency emphasized in NEP, 2006 requires that the services of environmental resources be given economic value, and such value to count equally with the economic values of other goods and services, in analysis of alternative courses of action. On the other hand, the Environment (Protection) Act, 1986 is an Act to provide for the protection and improvement of environment and for matters connected there with. The Water (Prevention and Control of Pollution) Act is an Act to provide for the prevention and control of water pollution and the maintaining or restoring of wholesomeness of water. Similarly, the Air (Prevention & Control of Pollution) Act, 1981 is an Act to provide for the prevention, control and abatement of air pollution. India's pollution prevention and control policy regime is characterized by "prohibit and punish" regime or "command and control" regime. Economic instruments, of which a large, feasible suite, has emerged through practical experience in several developed and developing countries, work by aligning the interests of economic actors with environmental compliance, primarily through application of "polluter pays". NEP, 2006 states that in future, accordingly, a judicious mix of incentives and fiats based regulatory instruments would be considered for each specific regulatory situation.

The second chapter mainly reviews the basic approaches to Environmental Policy in general adopted in various Countries in the form of Eco-tax, Subsidies; Pollution Permits, Refundable Deposits for Pollution control, Allocation of Property Rights, Government Investment Programmes etc. From this it is clear that, introduction of direct EIs such as pollution charges and tradable pollution permits does not have a legal backing in India now and as the design and implementation of the instruments is information-intensive and requires capacity building.

Environmental and therefore green initiative legislation in India is under the purview of several Ministries and other government bodies, often with significant overlap in responsibility and oversight. The major Ministries and government bodies involved in those initiatives are: (i) Ministry of Environment, Forest and Climate Change (MoEF & CC) (ii) Ministry of Power (MoP) (iii) Ministry of New and Renewable Energy (MNRE) (iv) Ministry of Commerce and Industries (MCI) (v) Bureau of Energy Efficiency (BEE) (vi) Central Pollution Control Board (CPCB) and (vii) Bureau of Indian Standards (BIS). All these bodies have major roles in the development and implementation of blanket legislation like the Environment Protection Act (EPA), the Environment Conservation Act (ECA) and the National Mission on Enhanced Energy Efficiency (NMEEE). The second chapter explains in detail the key legislations related to Green initiatives of various Ministries and departments mentioned above including Eco-labeling Scheme initiated in India and various Green labels which are currently prevalent in India.

Economic activities either affect or are affected by natural and environmental resources. Economic activities such as extraction, processing, manufacture, transport, consumption and disposal, change the stock of natural resources, add stress to environmental systems and introduce wastes to environmental media. Moreover, present economic activities affect the stock of natural resources available for the future and have inter-temporal welfare effects. As a result, the productivity of an economic system depends in part on both supply and quality of natural and environmental resources. Thus, economic management impacts on the environment and environmental quality impacts on efficient working of the economy. Environmental degradation imposes costs on the economy which results in output and human capital losses. The third chapter mainly concentrates on the theoretical explanation of Sustainable Development which include economy-environment linkages, definition of Sustainable Development and its explanation, components of Sustainable Development, rules of Sustainable Development and on how to realize Sustainable Development. The second part of this Chapter mainly focus on "India and Sustainable Development- MoEF & CC Initiatives" which explains in detail MoEF&CC's vision towards Sustainable Development, vision of the Ministry for the XIIth Plan, recent Initiatives in addressing Pollution, initiatives in addressing Climate Change, addressing Bio-diversity related challenges, monitorable socio-economic targets and goals in XIIth Plan and finally India's Stand in Rio+20 summit.

The fourth chapter conveys that our environment is under attack since advent of industrial revolution. The inexorable decay and degeneration in quality of environment was matter of serious concern and sought to overcome through command–and-control approach in beginning of 1970s. However, efforts to save environment has proved to be inadequate. This approach was focused on controlling industrial pollution but later witnessed paradigm shift in this direction after Rio Earth Summit. Sustainability has become guiding principles to emerging recalcitrant environment problems such as climate change and ozone depletion.

There has been growing realization that Market Based Instruments (MBIs) such as ecological tax (eco tax) are much better tool available to policy makers to regulate behavior of individuals/firms towards environment. It is based on "polluters pay" principle and provide incentives to polluters to change their behaviours and done away with costly monitoring by the government or state agencies. This chapter examines introduction of eco taxes in OECD countries which is being used in conjunction with command-or-control approach or in preference to it. This tax is being levied on energy, carbon emission, vehicle, congestion, water pollution, batteries, logging, tyres, beverage container, toxic waste levy, plastic bags, groundwater extraction, pesticides, landfill, ozone depletion, etc. It also examines effectiveness of eco taxes in controlling carbon emission, waste, etc. This chapter concludes by mentioning that why eco tax became one of popular mechanism to control environmental pollution, which was pioneered by Nordic countries but later followed by members of OECD countries. This chapter clearly establishes that introduction of eco tax unleashes possibility of double dividend- benefits by both a reduction in environmentally harmful activities and a reduction in conventional taxation.

Subsequent to discussion on environmental regulation in OECD countries, which clearly establishes that they are resorting to market based institutions (MBI) like eco taxes to protect the environment, this chapter explores the possibility of scope of eco taxes in India. It begins with stating that Indian environmental regulation has been predominantly rooted in command-and-control regime. This regime has not been able to control pollution in pursuance of its development activities. Environmental challenges are persistently increasing the pressure on governments to look ways to mitigate environmental damage while minimizing harm to economic activities. It is in this background, the last chapter argues that under prevailing constitutional and legal framework in India, it can be imposed by the central government as part of Union budget (Finance Act) under constitutional provisions of article 110, 246, 252 and 265. Alternatively, it may also be introduced under the Environment (Protection) Act, 1986.

By emulating the success of eco tax in OECD countries, India can impose this tax on water effluents, air pollution, vehicles, congestion, waste management, IT wastes, aggregates (sand, gravel and rock). Central government has already imposed Clean Energy Cess as a duty of excise on coal, lignite and peat to create National Clean Energy Fund (NCEF). The revenues generated for NCEF may, be preferably utilised for setting up infrastructure units for coal washing, for selective mining, and for identifying activities for gainful utilisation of coal ash. Besides this chapter also showcases small initiatives and steps of several State governments towards imposing eco taxes to regulate environment.

CHAPTER -1

APPROACHES IN ENVIRONMENT POLICY

(I) National Environment Policy (NEP), 2006

(i) Introduction

Approaches to Environment Policy vary in different Countries. The first part of this chapter reviews the policies adopted in India towards protection of environment and abatement of pollution. The National Environment Policy (NEP), 2006 is such a policy intended to be a guide to action in regulatory reform, programmes and projects for environmental conservation; and review and enactment of legislation, by agencies of the Central, State, and Local Governments. The Principle of economic efficiency emphasised in NEP,2006 requires that the services of environmental resources be given economic value, and such value to count equally with the economic values of other goods and services, in analysis of alternative courses of action. On the other hand, the Environment (Protection) Act, 1986 is an Act to provide for the protection and improvement of environment and for matters connected there with. The Water (Prevention and Control of Pollution) Act is an Act to provide for the prevention and control of water pollution and the maintaining or restoring of wholesomeness of water. Similarly, the Air (Prevention and Control of Pollution) Act, 1981 is an Act to provide for the prevention, control and abatement of air pollution. India's pollution prevention and control policy regime is characterised by "prohibit and punish" regime or "command and control" regime. Economic instruments, of which a large, feasible suite, has emerged through practical experience in several developed and developing countries, work by aligning the interests of economic actors with environmental compliance, primarily through application of "polluter pays". NEP, 2006 states that in future, accordingly, a judicious mix of incentives and fiats based regulatory instruments would be considered for each specific regulatory situation. The second part of this chapter mainly reviews the basic approaches to Environmental Policy in general adopted in various Countries in the form of Eco-tax, Subsidies, Pollution Permits, Refundable Deposits for Pollution control, Allocation of Property Rights, Government Investment Programmes etc. From this it is clear that, introduction of direct EIs such as pollution charges and tradable pollution permits does not have a legal backing in India now and as the design and implementation of the instruments is information-intensive and requires capacity building.

The National Environment Policy is a response to our national commitment to a clean environment, mandated in the Constitution in Articles 48 A and 51 A (g), strengthened by judicial interpretation of Article 21. It is recognised that maintaining a healthy environment is not the state's responsibility alone, but also that of every citizen. A spirit of partnership should thus be realised throughout the spectrum of environmental management in the country. While the state must galvanize its efforts, there should also be recognition by each individual - natural or institutional, of its responsibility towards maintaining and enhancing the quality of the environment.

The National Environment Policy has been motivated by

the above considerations and is intended to mainstream environmental concerns in all development activities. It briefly describes the key environmental challenges currently and prospectively facing the country, the objectives of environment policy, normative principles underlying policy action, strategic themes for intervention, broad indications of the legislative and institutional development needed to accomplish the strategic themes, and mechanisms for implementation and review. It has been prepared through a process of extensive consultation with experts, as well as diverse stakeholders, and this process is also documented.

The National Environment Policy is intended to be a guide to action in regulatory reform, programmes and projects for environmental conservation; and review and enactment of legislation, by agencies of the Central, State, and Local Governments. The dominant theme of this policy is that while conservation of environmental resources is necessary to secure livelihoods and well-being of all, the most secure basis for conservation is to ensure that people dependent on particular resources obtain better livelihoods from the fact of conservation, than from degradation of the resource

The policy also seeks to stimulate partnerships of different stakeholders, i.e. public agencies, local communities, academic and scientific institutions, the investment community, and international development partners, in harnessing their respective resources and strengths for environmental management.

(ii) The Principle of Economic Efficiency emphasised in NEP 2006

In various public actions for environmental conservation, economic efficiency would be sought to be realised .This Principle requires that the services of environmental resources be given economic value, and such value to count equally with the economic values of other goods and services, in analysis of alternative courses of action. Further implications of this Principle are as follows:

Polluter Pays: Impacts of acts of production and consumption of one party may be visited on third parties who do not have a direct economic nexus with the original act. Such impacts are termed "externalities". If the costs (or benefits) of the externalities are not re-visited on the party responsible for the original act, the resulting level of the entire sequence of production or consumption, and externality, is inefficient. In such a situation, economic efficiency may be restored by making the perpetrator of the externality bear the cost (or benefit) of the same.

The policy will, accordingly, promote the internalisation of environmental costs, including through the use of incentives based policy instruments, taking into account the approach that the polluter should, in principle, bear the cost of pollution, with due regard to the public interest, and without distorting international trade and investment.

Cost Minimisation: Where the environmental benefits of a course of action cannot, for methodological or conceptual reasons, be imputed economic value (as in the case of "Incomparable Entities", in any event the economic costs of realizing the benefits should be minimised. Efficiency of resource use may also be accomplished by the use of policy instruments that create incentives to minimise wasteful use and consumption of natural resources. The principle of efficiency also applies to issues of environmental governance by streamlining processes and procedures in order to minimise costs and delays.

Land Degradation: The degradation of land, through soil erosion, alkali-salinisation, water logging, pollution, and reduction in organic matter content has several proximate and underlying causes. The proximate causes include loss of forest and tree cover (leading to erosion by surface water run-off and winds), unsustainable grazing, excessive use of irrigation (in many cases without proper drainage, leading to leaching of sodium and potassium salts), improper use of agricultural chemicals (leading to accumulation of toxic chemicals in the soil), diversion of animal wastes for domestic fuel (leading to reduction in soil nitrogen and organic matter), and disposal of industrial and domestic wastes on productive land.

These proximate causes of land degradation in turn, are driven by implicit and explicit subsidies for water, power, fertiliser and pesticides. Grazing lands are usually common property resources, and insufficient empowerment of local institutions for their management leads to overexploitation of the biomass base. The absence of conducive policies and persistence of certain regulatory practices reduces people's incentives for afforestation, and leads to reduced levels of green cover. It is essential that the relevant fiscal, tariffs, and sectoral policies take explicit account of their unintentional impacts on land degradation, if the fundamental basis of livelihoods for the vast majority of our people is not to be irreparably damaged.

(iii) Use of Economic Principles in Environmental Decision-making:

It is necessary that the costs associated with the degradation and depletion of natural resources be incorporated into the decisions of economic actors at various levels, to reverse the tendency to treat these resources as "free goods" and to pass the costs of degradation to other sections of society, or to future generations of the country.

At the macro-level, a system of natural resource accounting is required to assess whether in the course of economic growth we are drawing down, or enhancing, the natural resource base of production, including relevant depletable assets. In addition, the environmental costs and benefits associated with various activities, including sectoral policies, should be evaluated to ensure that these factors are duly taken into account in decision-making.

The current near exclusive reliance on fiats based instruments for environmental regulation do not permit individual actors to minimise their own costs of compliance. This leads, on the one hand, to noncompliance in many cases, and on the other, unnecessary diversion of societal resources from other pressing needs. Economic instruments, of which a large, feasible suite, has emerged through practical experience in several developed and developing countries, work by aligning the interests of economic actors with environmental compliance, primarily through application of "polluter pays". This may ensure that for any given level of environmental quality desired, the society-wide costs of meeting the standard are minimised. However, in some cases, use of economic instruments may require intensive monitoring, which too may entail significant societal costs. On the other hand, use of existing policy instruments, such as the fiscal regime, may significantly reduce or eliminate the need for enhanced institutional capacities to administer the incentive based instruments. In future, accordingly, a judicious mix of incentives and fiats based regulatory instruments would be considered for each specific regulatory situation.

(iv) Action Plan emphasised in NEP, 2006

(a) Strengthen, including through capacity building, the initiatives, taken by the Central Statistical Organisation in the area of natural resource accounting, with a view to its adoption in the system of national income accounts. Further strengthen in all respects, the system of collection, collation and analysis of all significant and relevant environmental monitoring data.

(b) Develop and promote the use of standardised environmental accounting practices and norms in preparation of statutory financial statements for large industrial enterprises, in order to encourage greater environmental responsibility in investment decision-making, management practices, and public scrutiny.

(c) Encourage financial institutions to adopt appropriate appraisal practices, so that environmental risks are adequately considered in the financing of projects.

(d) Facilitate the integration of environmental values into cost-benefit analysis, to encourage more efficient allocation of resources while making public investment decisions.

(e) Prepare and implement an action plan on the use of economic instruments for environmental regulation in specified contexts, including those relating to unsustainable production and consumption.

(f) Consider creation of a National Environment Restoration Fund from the net proceeds of economic instruments, user fees for access to specified natural resources, and voluntary contributions. The Fund may be used for restoration of environmental resources, including clean-up of toxic and hazardous waste legacies.

(v) Conclusion

India's pollution prevention and control policy regime is characterised by "prohibit and punish" regime or "command and control" regime [Sankar (1999)]. In this regime, penalties are not proportional to the extent of violation from the standards. Enforcement of the laws is also weak. The major factor inhibiting the introduction of Economic Instruments (EIs) is that all the pollution prevention and control legislations come under criminal law.

The National Environmental Policy (NEP), 2006 recognises this problem. It states that the present environmental mechanism is predominantly based on doctrines of criminal liability, which have not proved sufficiently effective, and need to be supplemented. It notes that, civil law offers flexibility, and its sanctions can be more effectively tailored to particular situations. The evidentiary burdens of civil proceedings are less daunting than those of criminal law. It also allows for preventive policing through orders and injunctions.

The NEP recommends a review of the existing legislations to arrive at a judicious mix of civil and criminal processes and sanctions. It states that civil liability law, civil sanctions, and processes would govern most situations of non-compliance. Criminal processes and sanctions would be available for serious, and potentially provable, infringements of environmental law, and their initiation would be vested in responsible authorities. Recourse may also be had to the relevant provisions in the Indian Penal Code and the Criminal Procedure Code. Both civil and criminal penalties would be graded according to the severity of the infraction.

The NEP notes that EIs, work by aligning the interest of economic actors with environmental compliance, primarily through application of "polluter pays" principle and recommends an action plan for preparation and implementation on the use of EIs for environmental regulation in specified contexts.

As introduction of direct EIs such as pollution charges and tradable pollution permits does not have a legal backing now and as the design and implementation of the instruments is information-intensive and requires capacity building.

(II)The Environment (Protection) Act, 1986

(a) Introduction

The Environment (Protection) Act, 1986 is an Act to provide for the protection and improvement of environment and for matters connected there with. The decisions were taken at the United Nations Conference on the Human Environment held at Stockholm in June, 1972, in which India participated, to take appropriate steps for the protection and improvement of human environment.

Thus it was considered necessary further to implement the decisions aforesaid in so far as they relate to the protection and improvement of environment and the prevention of hazards to human beings, other living creatures, plants and property.

(b) The powers of Central Government to take measures to protect and improve Environment under this are as follows

Subject to the provisions of this Act, the Central Government shall have the power to take all such measures as it deems necessary or expedient for the purpose of protecting and improving the quality of the environment and preventing controlling and abating environmental pollution. In particular, and without prejudice to the generality of the provisions of above power, such measures may include measures with respect to all or any of the following matters, namely:--

(i) co-ordination of actions by the State Governments, officers and other authorities--

  (a) under this Act, or the rules made there under, or

  (b) under any other law for the time being in force which is relatable to the objects of this Act;

(ii) planning and execution of a nation-wide programme for the prevention, control and abatement of environmental pollution;

(iii) laying down standards for the quality of environment in its various aspects;

(iv) laying down standards for emission or discharge of environmental pollutants from various sources whatsoever: provided that different standards for emission or discharge may be laid down under this clause from different sources having regard to the quality or composition of the emission or discharge of environmental pollutants from such sources;

(v) restriction of areas in which any industries, operations or processes or class of industries, operations or processes shall not be carried out or shall be carried out subject to certain safeguards;

(vi) laying down procedures and safeguards for the prevention of accidents which may cause environmental pollution and remedial measures for such accidents;

(vii) laying down procedures and safeguards for the handling of hazardous substances;

(viii) examination of such manufacturing processes, materials and substances as are likely to cause environmental pollution;

(ix) carrying out and sponsoring investigations and research relating to problems of environmental pollution;

(x) inspection of any premises, plant, equipment, machinery, manufacturing or other processes, materials or substances and giving, by order, of such directions to such authorities, officers or persons as it may consider necessary to take steps for the prevention, control and abatement of environmental pollution;

(xi) establishment or recognition of environmental laboratories and institutes to carry out the functions entrusted to such environmental laboratories and institutes under this Act;

(xii) collection and dissemination of information in respect of matters relating to environmental pollution;

(xiii) preparation of manuals, codes or guides relating to the prevention, control and abatement of environmental pollution;

(xiv) such other matters as the Central Government deems necessary or expedient for the purpose of securing the effective implementation of the provisions of this Act.

The Central Government may, if it considers it necessary or expedient so to do for the purpose of this Act, by order, published in the Official Gazette, constitute an authority or authorities by such name or names as may be specified in the order for the purpose of exercising and performing such of the powers and functions (including the power to issue directions under section 5) of the Central

Government under this Act and for taking measures with respect to such of the matters referred to in sub-section (2) as may be mentioned in the order and subject to the supervision and control of the Central Government and the provisions of such order, such authority or authorities may exercise and powers or perform the functions or take the measures so mentioned in the order as if such authority or authorities had been empowered by this Act to exercise those powers or perform those functions or take such measures.

(III) The Water (Prevention and Control of Pollution) Act, 1974

This is an Act to provide for the prevention and control of water pollution and the maintaining or restoring of wholesomeness of water, for the establishment, with a view to carrying out the purposes aforesaid, of Boards for the prevention and control of water pollution, for conferring on and assigning to such Boards powers and functions relating thereto and for matters connected therewith. It is expedient to provide for the prevention and control of water pollution and the maintaining or restoring of wholesomeness of water, for the establishment, with a view to carrying out the purposes aforesaid, of Boards for the prevention and control of water pollution and for conferring on and assigning to such Boards powers and functions relating thereto. Parliament has no power to make laws for the States with respect to any of the matters aforesaid except as provided in articles 249 and 250 of the Constitution. In pursuance of clause (1) of article 252 of the Constitution, resolutions have been passed by all the Houses of the Legislatures of the States of Assam, Bihar, Gujarat, Haryana, Himachal Pradesh, Jammu and Kashmir, Karnataka, Kerala, Madhya Pradesh, Rajasthan, Tripura and West Bengal to the effect that the matters aforesaid should be regulated in those States by Parliament by law.

(IV) The Water (Prevention and Control of Pollution) Cess Act, 1977

This Act of Parliament received the assent of the President on the 7th December, 1977, and is an Act to provide for the levy and collection of a cess on water consumed by persons carrying on certain industries and by local authorities, with a view to augment the resources of the Central Board and the State Boards for the prevention and control of water pollution constituted under the Water (Prevention and Control of Pollution) Act, 1974.

Levy and collection of Cess

(1) There shall be levied and collected a cess for the purpose of the Water (Prevention and Control of Pollution) Act, 1974 (6 of 1974) and utilisation there under.

(2) The cess under sub-section (1) shall be payable by--

   (a) Every person carrying on any specified industry; and

   (b) Every local authority,

and shall be calculated on the basis of water consumed by such person or local authority, as the case may be, for any of the purposes specified in column (1) of Schedule II, at such rate, not exceeding the rate specified in the corresponding entry in column (2) thereof, as the Central Government may, by notification in the Official Gazette, from time to time, specify. Where any person carrying on any specified industry or any local authority consuming water for domestic purpose liable to pay cess fails to comply with any of the provisions of section 25 of the Water (Prevention and Control of Pollution) Act, 1974 (6 of 1974) or an of the standards laid so down by the Central Government under the Environment (Protection) Act, 1986, cess shall be and payable at such rate, not exceeding the rate specified in column (3) of Schedule II, as the Central Government may, by notification in the Official Gazette, from time to time specify.

(V) The Air (Prevention and Control of Pollution) Act, 1981

The Air (Prevention and Control of Pollution) Act, 1981 is an Act to provide for the prevention, control and abatement of air pollution, for the establishment, with a view to carrying out the aforesaid purposes, of Boards, for conferring on and assigning to such Boards powers and functions relating thereto and for matters connected therewith. Decisions were taken at the United Nations Conference on the Human Environment held in Stockholm in June, 1972, in which India participated, to take appropriate steps for the preservation of the natural resources of the earth which, among other things, include the preservation of the quality of air and control of air pollution. Thus it was considered necessary to implement the decisions aforesaid in so far as they relate to the preservation of the quality of air and control of air pollution.

(VI) The National Green Tribunal (NGT) Act, 2010

This Act of Parliament received assent of the President on the 2nd June, 2010, and is an Act to provide for the establishment of a National Green Tribunal for the effective and expeditious disposal of cases relating to environmental protection and conservation of forests and other natural resources including enforcement of any legal right relating to environment and giving relief and compensation for damages to persons and property and for matters connected therewith or incidental thereto. India is a party to the decisions taken at the United Nations Conference on the human Environment held at Stockholm in June, 1972, in which India participated, calling upon the States to take appropriate steps for the protection and improvement of the human environment. Decisions were taken at the United Nations Conference on Environment and Development held at Rio de Janeiro in June, 1992, in which India participated, calling upon the States to provide effective access to judicial and administrative proceedings, including redress and remedy and to develop national laws regarding liability and compensation for the victims of pollution and other environmental damage. In the judicial pronouncement in India, the right to healthy environment has been construed as a part of the right to life under article 21 of the Constitution. It is considered expedient to implement the decisions taken at the aforesaid conferences and to have a National Green Tribunal in view of the involvement of multi-disciplinary issues relating to the environment.

As per the National Green Tribunal (NGT) Act , 2010; the Central Government by notification, established with effect from such date as may specified therein, a Tribunal to be known as the National Green Tribunal to exercise the jurisdiction, powers and authority conferred on such Tribunal by or under this Act. The Tribunal was established for speedy disposal of environmental cases. The Tribunal consist of- (a) a full time Chairperson; (b) not less than ten but subject to maximum of twenty full time Judicial Members as the Central Government may, from time to time, notify; (c) not less than ten but subject to maximum of twenty full time Expert Members, as the Central Government may, from time to time, notify.

(VII) Basic Approaches to Environmental Policy in General.

(i) Introduction

Pollution is the introduction of contaminants into the natural environment that cause adverse change. Pollution can take the form of chemical substances or energy, such as noise, heat or light. Pollutants, the components of pollution, can be either foreign substances/energies or naturally occurring contaminants. Pollution is often classed as point source or non-point source pollution.

The major forms of pollution are listed below along with the particular contaminant relevant to each of them:

- Air pollution: - The release of chemicals and particulates into the atmosphere. Common gaseous pollutants include carbon monoxide, sulfur dioxide, chlorofluorocarbons (CFCs) and nitrogen oxides produced by industry and motor vehicles. Photochemical ozone and smog are created as nitrogen oxides and hydrocarbons react to sunlight. Particulate matter, or fine dust is characterised by their micrometer size PM10 to PM2.5.
- Light pollution:- includes light trespass, over -illumination and astronomical interference.
- Littering: - the criminal throwing of inappropriate man-made objects, unremoved, onto public and private properties.
- Noise pollution: - which encompasses roadway noise, aircraft noise, industrial noise as well as high-intensity sonar.
- Soil contamination occurs when chemicals are released by spill or underground leakage. Among the most significant soil contaminants are hydrocarbons, heavy metals, pesticides and chlorinated hydrocarbons.
- Radioactive contamination, resulting from 20th century activities in atomic physics, such as nuclear power generation and nuclear weapons research, manufacture and deployment.
- Thermal pollution is a temperature change in natural water bodies caused by human influence, such as use of water as coolant in a power plant.
- Visual pollution, which can refer to the presence of overhead power lines, motorway billboards, scarred landforms (as from strip mining), open storage of trash, municipal solid waste or space debris.
- Water pollution, by the discharge of wastewater from commercial and industrial waste (intentionally or through spills) into surface waters; discharges of untreated domestic sewage, and chemical contaminants, such as chlorine, from treated sewage; release of waste and contaminants into surface runoff flowing to surface waters (including urban

runoff and agricultural runoff, which may contain chemical fertilisers and pesticides); waste disposal and leaching into groundwater; eutrophication and littering.

Pollution is likely to be with us in some from or other since all production involves pollution in one form or another. Zero pollution implies zero production. What is required is a package of measures to identify and monitor pollutant, to identify their economic, ecological and sociological effects and to confine them within levels which are not only safe for survival but fully appropriate to the quality of life expected. This involves a choice between two things: economic growth and the carrying capacity of the environment. The objective of economic growth depletes natural resources on a vast and increasing scale, which can be avoided by working on ecological principles, with economic growth redirected to embrace the overall quality of life.

In broad terms four general methods have been proposed for the control of activities that damage the environment.

(A) Moral suasion, which is an appeal to reduce pollution in the broader interests of the society.

(B) Regulation or direct control requiring polluters to cut back their emissions to maintain a certain level of environmental quality or to install a specified treatment of procedures.

(C) An effluent charge or pollution tax

(D) Subsidies

(E) Refundable deposits

(F) Pollution permits, and

(G) Allocation of property rights

(H) Government investment programmes.

(A) Moral Suasion

Moral suasion (a phrase from the Latin words "moral" and "suasion" which denote respectively "conduct or character that is right and virtuous" and "to present in a pleasing manner" - sometimes known as jawboning), is defined in the economic sphere as "the attempt to coerce private economic activity via governmental exhortation in directions not already defined or dictated by existing statute law. The 'moral' aspect comes from the pressure for 'moral responsibility' to operate in a way that is consistent with furthering the good of the economy.

There are two types of moral suasion:

1. "Pure" moral suasion refers to an appeal for altruistic behaviour and is rarely used in economic policy
2. "Impure" moral suasion, or simply "moral suasion", is backed by explicit or implicit threats by authorities in order to provide incentives to comply with their wishes

Moral suasion differs from direct suasion using laws and regulations in that penalty for non-compliance are not systematically assessed on non compliers. This has led some authors to criticise moral suasion as immoral, since compliers get penalised for cooperating with the stated government agenda (thus incurring extra costs) while non-compliers are not punished. Other objections to the use of moral suasion include the fact that it constitutes extra-legal coercion by the government, that it adds uncertainty to the regulatory process, and that it can undermine or delay the implementation of effective legislation.

Usage of moral suasion in environment regulation consists in making polluters feel responsible for the negative externalities that they cause. Moral suasion can be very efficient from an economic standpoint since economic agents are free to use any cost-minimising solution deal with their negative externalities instead of having to rely on a government-prescribed regulation or tax. Furthermore, the administrative costs of using moral suasion to deal with environmental problems are very low. Marine debris regulations in the United States (1989-1993) revealed that moral suasion can be an effective tool to limit the discharge of trash into water in spite the offenders' low probability of being detected. The evidence on the effectiveness of moral suasion methods to induce environmentally desirable behaviour however is not strong unless it is coupled with other instruments. For example, Canadian policy makers advocates for moral suasion in their endeavour to achieve environmental and wildlife policy objectives, a course of action likely to fail if little regard is placed on the accompanying incentives.

Moral Suasion refers to voluntary programmes such as non-mandatory investment in pollution control equipment by firms that decide to act in a manner that meets their social responsibilities or voluntary collection of trash or garbage by households who deliver them to collection centers for recycling. Voluntary trash recycling programmes, voluntary use of unleaded and low lead gasoline, sales of auto emission control kits, car pooling, and energy saving programmes are some of the popular voluntary programmes in practice in US. However, the success of these programmes to control pollution is to a great extent influenced by strength of the population willing to participate in such programmes. Hence where the problem of pollution is high and substantial improvement in environmental quality is posing a problem, direct controls and price incentives are more efficient.

Despite these limitations, voluntary programmes have useful roles. Firstly, where the fiscal processes of a country fails to generate enough funds for the maintenance of environmental quality, voluntary programmes can be relied upon. This is the state in majority of the low income and lower-middle income group countries, where public activities like school and hospital are subject to under financing, to such an extent that financing of environmental protection is assigned the lowest priority. Secondly, voluntarism can be helpful in instances where the activities that damage the environment have to be detected and monitored i.e., where polluters have to be identified and level of pollution has to be metered. A third and potentially important role for voluntary measures arises when there are sudden and unexpected episodes of pollution perhaps due to a gas-leak or so. The role played by the voluntary groups during Bhopal tragedy in relief works is clear evidence to this merit of voluntary programmes. Voluntary programmes, hence, have an important role to play in the protection of environmental quality particularly in brief unexpected emergencies or where effective surveillance is impossible.

(B) Regulation or Direct Control

This takes two forms: a, imposition of legal ceilings on the amount any polluter is permitted to emit/discharge. For example, in India, Minimum National Standards (MINAS) for waste water discharges and emission standards for several industries have been fixed by the Central Board for Prevention and Control of Water Pollution and Air Pollution. Unto 1986, MINAS was finalised for thirteen water polluting industries. Specification of how particular activity must be carried on - for example, direct control may require industries to install an Electro Static Precipitator (ESP) or scrubbers to capture some of the emission of the polluting firm. In some of the western countries, direct regulations prohibit backyard incinerators or the use of high sulphur coal. Direct control may also specify the stack height of the polluting firm.

The first type of the direct control, prescribing a standard for the environmental media or fixing a ceiling on the quantity of effluents / emission requires that it should be possible to measure the volume of waste emission of the polluter. Direct control is particularly significant in cases of pollution involving highly hazardous pollutants. In case of pollutants like cyanide, even a small quantity of which has serious consequences on health of human beings (as well as animals and other living organisms), direct control should be used to totally prohibit their discharge altogether.

In spite of the above merits exclusive reliance on direct control has not been reliable and successful in practice. It has been criticised on grounds that it does not provoke and promote incentive to innovate equipments that will control pollution more efficiently. Further, direct control can be effective only when the fine it imposes on the polluter for non-compliance with the regulation is sufficiently high.

(C) Taxes (say Eco-tax)

Eco-tax (short for Ecological taxation) refers to taxes intended to promote ecologically sustainable activities via economic incentives. Such a policy can complement or avert the need for regulatory (command and control) approaches. Often, an Eco-tax policy proposal may attempt to maintain overall tax revenue by proportionately reducing other taxes (e.g. taxes on human labour and renewable resources); such proposals are known as a green tax shift towards ecological taxation. Ecotaxes are examples of Pigouvian taxes, which are taxes that attempt to make the private parties involved, feel the social burden of their actions.

A tax on pollution requires the polluter to install a meter that registers the effluents/emissions released from the production process in the same way as a meter records the consumption of electricity and water. In accordance with the level of emissions/effluents, the firm will be charged. Thus, the higher the level of wastes discharged by a firm, the higher will be the tax bill for the firm and a firm can reduce its tax bill by polluting less. One form of a pollution tax is the residual charge or waste disposal tax or effluent charge. An effluent charge is the price that the polluters have to pay for the opportunity to discharge wastes into environment. If the polluters are not subject to any effluent charge, i.e. , if they do not have to pay at all for the discharge of the firm's wastes, then it means that the price for opportunities of polluting is zero.

Pollution charges are considered to be more effective and more reliable than direct controls. They are automatic, certain and promote incentives to innovate cheaper costs of pollution control (because it will reduce pollution control cost for the firm). Besides pollution tax is held by economists as the least cost method for achieving pollution control. Besides these, the crucial point is that a pollution tax is said to promote that equal distribution of the burden of pollution control cost on all firms i.e., a pollution tax is more equitable than direct control.

In spite of the merits claimed in favour of an effluent tax like dependability, permanence, efficiency, economy and equity, there are three objections to a pollution tax. The first of these come from the industrialists who sometimes say that a residual charge would impose an 'unfair double burden' on the industry. The industrialists argue that they will have to pay the tax and at the same time incur expenditure on installing pollution abatement equipment. Secondly, consumers object to a pollution tax on grounds that the industry would pass on the burden of charge on them in the form of higher product prices. A third objection to a pollution tax is from environmentalists, who consider it as a license to pollute. The environmentalists claim that the polluters should pay compensation to the victims and not taxes to the Government.

(D) Subsidies

Subsidies are already in use. The advocates of subsidies say that financial inducement can be just as effective when they take form of a reward for good behaviour than in the form of penalty (tax). Subsidies take following two forms:

1. Partial payment of the cost of installation of the some sort of pollution control equipment.
2. The offer of a fixed reward for every reduction in emissions from some base level, usually some amount that the polluter used to emit in the past.

Subsidies mostly cover a part of the investment on pollution control equipment. From the year 1983-84, the Indian Government offers a grant of investment allowance at a rate of thirty-five per cent of the actual cost of new machinery or plant that would facilitate control of pollution. Subsides for the purchase of equipment sometimes take the form of outright grants - for example, for the installation and operation of a treatment plant. Often the subsidies offered to private firms for the installation of pollution control equipment take the form of tax incentive rather than direct government payments. For example, the Central Board for the Prevention and Control of the Water Pollution in India offers a rebate of seven per cent of the cess payable by polluting industries under the Water (Prevention and Control of Pollution) Cess Act, if it installs any plant for treatment of trade effluents. A subsidy based or quantity of emission reduced, producers the same effect as a tax for an individual polluter. In both cases, the more he emits, the worse off he is financially, because he either receives a smaller subsidy or a higher tax bill.

Tax on polluting output raises cost. Subsidies add to output and net profits of the firm while a pollution tax decreases. Secondly, the enforcement of subsidy scheme poses administrative problem, when subsidy is paid for every reduction in pollution beyond a certain level, it is necessary that a bench mark must be established from which reduction are to be measured. Finally a tax on pollution generates revenue while a subsidy is demand for revenue from public treasure.

(E) Pollution Permits

Third type of financial inducement strongly recommended by many economists is the sale of pollution permits. Under this, the environmental authority determines the maximum amount of a specific type of pollution per unit of time that is within safe limits - that is consistent with the community's environmental objective - and then issues a batch of permits authorizing (altogether) just that amount of pollution. Each permit could give its owner the "right" to pollute up to specified amount in a given place during a particular period of time. These permits are offered for sale in an organised market where its price is determined by its supply and demand. The supply curve would be a vertical line since the total number of permits issued at any time is fixed, while the demand curve is downward sloping.

It reduces the uncertainly about the quantity that will be emitted into the community. Under a tax rate, the quantity of emissions depends on the response of the polluting firm to the tax rate imposed. On the other hand, in the case of pollution permits, the ceiling on emission is determined in advance by the environmental authority which enforces this ceiling by issuing a specified number of permits that would allow only that total quantity of emissions already decided. Secondly, pollution permits are invulnerable to inflation, and work effectively even as population and industrial activity increase. This is because; their price will automatically increase following increases in pollution and industrial activity. Similarly when the impact of pollution varies between locations, number of permits issued in each location can be varied depending on the impact of pollution. For example, in an area more vulnerable to pollution, fewer permits may be sold by decision. In spite of these advantages, pollution permits lack political appeal. For the operation of both taxes and permits, however, the source of pollution must be identified. Where it is not possible, only an alternative method of control can work.

(F) Use of Refundable Deposits for Pollution control

Robert Solow and Edwin Mills have suggested the method of using a refundable deposit for pollution in cases where it is not possible to monitor, observe and detect environmental damage. In this case it is required to leave an appropriate deposit with environmental authorities who can pay an interest on all such deposits. The funds may be used by the environmental authorities for its environmental protection activities but must be refunded to the polluter in case he ceases his activities that cause pollution.

(G) Allocation of Property Rights

Allocation of property rights is a method that protects the environmental resources by putting them into the hands of private individual who consequently have a financial stake in their preservation. It is suggested that if exclusive property rights are defined for such resources, the public-good environmental quality can be transformed into a private good and optimal environmental allocation will be reached. Government intervention is needed only in assigning environmental property titles. With property rights adequately defined, market will find the correct allocation.

A property right can be defined as a set of rules specifying the use of scarce resources and goods. The set of rules include obligation and rights. Prof. Dales has distinguished four types of property rights.

1. Exclusive property rights that cover the right of disposal and the right to destroy the resources, notably the right of sale. Even such exclusive property rights are controlled by a set of rules which protect other individuals or maintain economic values. For example, city zoning laws.
2. Status or functional ownership refers to a set of rules limited to a specific person or status. In such cases right to use an object or to receive a service is not transferable.
3. Third, rights to use a public utility (such as a highway) or a public good (a national park) relate to a specific use.
4. Common property resources with no exclusion defined.

Coase theorem which states that in the absence of transaction costs, bargaining among different users of the environment will result in a Pareto optimal allocation of environment when exclusive (transferable) property rights to the environment are defined. The resulting allocation is independent of the initial distribution of property titles. The property rights approach can work only when the damage to the natural resources comes from a few sources that are easily identified and where private owners themselves cause environmental deterioration, this solution is not applicable.

(H) Government Investment Programmes

These include installation of waste treatment plants, slum-clearance, management of wild life refuges, reforestation and afforestation etc. Besides these the research Programmes and Programmes to create environmental awareness also are part of government investment programmes. The public good character of the environmental resources necessitates government's investment and participation to maintain and preserve environmental quality. The volume of financial resources needed for the most effective and efficient management of the environment may be too high for the private sector to appropriate. Hence active participation by the government is essential. There are thus various policy instruments available to control pollution and preserve environmental quality. New methods and concepts are also being developed along with new technologies to control pollution.

CHAPTER -2

GREEN INITIATIVES BY GOVERNMENT OF INIDA

Brief review of the Green Initiatives by Government of ndia

Environmental and therefore green initiative legislation in India is under the purview of several Ministries and other government bodies, often with significant overlap in responsibility and oversight. The major Ministries and government bodies involved in those initiatives are:

1. Ministry of Environment, Forest and Climate Change (MoEFand CC)
2. Ministry of Power (MoP)
3. Ministry of New and Renewable Energy (MNRE)
4. Ministry of Commerce and Industry (MCI)
5. Bureau of Energy Efficiency (BEE)
6. Central Pollution Control Board (CPCB)
7. Bureau of Indian Standards (BIS)

All these bodies have major roles in the development and implementation of blanket legislation like the Environment Protection Act (EPA), the Environment Conservation Act (ECA) and the National Mission on Enhanced Energy Efficiency (NMEEE).

(A) Ministry for Environment, Forest Climate Change (MoEF&CC)

The MoEF & CC is the nodal agency in the administrative structure of the Central Government for planning, promotion, co-ordination and oversight of the implementation of India's environmental policies and Programmes. The Ministry is primarily concerned with implementation of policies and programmes relating to conservation of the country's natural resources including lakes and rivers, bio-diversity, forests and wildlife, ensuring welfare of animals and prevention and abatement of pollution. The objectives are supported by necessary policy framework and legislative and regulatory measures aiming at preservation, conservation and protection of environment. Some of these are the National Forest Policy 1988, National Conservation Strategy and Policy Statement on Environment and Development, 1992, Policy Statement on Abatement of Pollution, 1992, and National Environment Policy 2006 and associated legislation, including the Forests (Conservation) Act, 1980, Air (Prevention and Control of Pollution) Act, 1981, Environment (Protection) (EPA)Act, 1986, Public Liability Insurance Act, 1991, National Environment Tribunal Act, 1995, National Environment Appellate Authority Act, 1997, Prevention of Cruelty to Animals Act, 2001, Bio-Diversity Act 2002 and National Green Tribunal Act, 2010.

Ministry has formulated various regulatory instruments (environmental standards, consent administration, authorisation, environmental and forestry clearances etc.) and created institutional infrastructure at the National, regional, and State level in the form of Regional Offices of the Ministry, Central Pollution Control Board, State Pollution Control Boards/ Pollution Control Committees, State Departments of Environment and Forest, and various environmental research institutions/ organisations etc. Ministry has also launched several Plan schemes to strengthen the regulatory mechanism for environmental management.

Pursuant to instructions from the Planning Commission and Ministry of Finance, a number of on-going Plan Schemes of the Ministry were consolidated/ merged into broad thematic schemes as a measure of rationalisation exercise carried out by the Ministry for the Eleventh Five Year Plan. In the process of further rationalisation of the Schemes, thematic Schemes have been further reduced from 22 to the following 18 Schemes, with each Scheme having further components/ programmes, in the Twelfth Five Year Plan:

(i) Environmental Monitoring and Governance

(ii) Pollution Abatement

(iii) Research and Development for Conservation and Development

(iv) Conservation of Natural Resources and Ecosystems

(v) Environmental Information, Education and Awareness

(vi) Climate Change Action Programme

(vii) International Cooperation Activities

(viii) National Coastal Management Programme

(ix) National River Conservation Plan

(x) Grants-in-aid to Forestry and Wildlife Institutions

(xi) Capacity building in Forestry Sector

(xii) Afforestation and Forest Management

(xiii) Strengthening of Forestry Division

(xiv) Strengthening of Wildlife Division

(xv) Wildlife Management

(xvi) Project Tiger

(xvii) National Afforestation and Eco Development Board

(xviii) Animal Welfare

Key legislation

The Ministry is the apex authority on environmental matters which makes it a very important part of any major environmental or energy efficiency regulation. As a result, the MoEF & CC is involved in many policies and initiatives on these subjects. This includes the EPA which was already explained in the introduction chapter of this book, and the Environment Impact Assessment (EIA) which were developed by the Ministry. The Ministry also is part of the steering committee for the Eco-mark labeling scheme in India. Other key policies that the Ministry is involved with include the Energy Conservation Building Code (ECBC), the ECA, the Emission codes, the National Action Plan on Climate Change (NAPCC) and its derivative policies and the proposed E-waste rules.

(a) Environment Impact Assessment

EIA is one of well-recognised management tools for incorporating environmental concerns in development projects at the planning stage. In India, environmental clearance has been made mandatory since January 1994 in respect of 32 developmental activities including industry, Thermal Power, Mining, River Valley and Infrastructure projects and new constructions and industrial estate projects. Environmental Clearance (EC) to developmental projects was accorded as per the procedure laid down in EIA Notification of 1994.

The Ministry has undertaken re-engineering of EC Process and issued an EIA Notification, 2006 as further amended in 2009. Under this Notification, developmental activities have been categorised into Categories 'A' and 'B' based on potential impacts instead of investment criteria. Category 'A' projects/ activities will be appraised at Central level by Expert Appraisal Committees (EACs) while Category 'B' projects/ activities will be appraised at State level by State-level Environmental Impact Assessment Authority (SEIAA).

To facilitate preparation of better quality of EIAs and for the benefit of all stakeholders, the Ministry has prepared sector-specific manuals for activities covered under the Schedule of EIA Notification, 2006 (also posted on Ministry's website). The sector-specific manuals, inter alia, include thermal power plants, refinery and petrochemical complexes, integrated steel plants, ports and harbours, mining and mineral sectors, coal washery, airports, etc.

For protecting the coastal environment, the Ministry had issued a Coastal Regulation Zone (CRZ) Notification in February 1991 for regulation of development in coastal zone areas. Based on experience of implementation of this Notification and taking into account the finding of the Report titled 'Final Frontier' by Prof. M.S. Swaminathan, a re-engineered CRZ Notification was issued in January 2011 for protection of livelihood of traditional communities, preservation of coastal ecology and sustainable development in coastal regions. This Notification includes the procedure for CRZ approval, with time lines, inclusion of water area upto 12 nautical mines in the sea, concept of hazard line to be demarcated over next five years, and special provisions for areas like Greater Mumbai, Goa, Kerala, etc. as well as designation of Critically Vulnerable Coastal Areas (CVCAs).

(b) Green India Mission (GIM)

The National Action Plan on Climate Change (NAPCC) launched by Government of India outlines the strategy and approach to be adopted to meet the challenge of the impact of climate change in India. It includes institutionalisation of eight National Missions such as National Solar Mission; National Mission for Enhanced Energy Efficiency; National Mission on Sustainable Habitat; National Water Mission; National Mission for Sustaining the Himalayan Ecosystem; National Mission for a "Green India"; National Mission for Sustainable Agriculture; National Mission on Strategic Knowledge for Climate Change. In this regard; the Ministry of Environment Forest & Climate Change had drafted a comprehensive Green India Mission (GIM) document through a consultative process involving relevant stakeholders, aimed at both increasing the forest and tree cover by 5 million hectare as well as increasing the quality of existing forest cover in another 5 million hectare. GIM envisages a holistic view of greening and focuses on multiple ecosystem services, especially, biodiversity, water, biomass, etc., with carbon sequestration as a co-benefit. GIM was approved by the Prime Minister's Council on Climate Change on 22nd February 2011.

GIM seeks to improve the quality of forest cover and create new forest cover using a landscape approach to achieve integrated actions on a "scale", which is also cross-sectoral involving stakeholders and various Departments, outcome-based monitoring, collabouration for research, development of a cadre of "community foresters" to facilitate field-level implementation, and participative models of community engagements which strengthen decentralised governance. Selection of landscapes would be based on a range of criteria, including projected vulnerability to climate change, areas with significant biodiversity and other ecosystem values, critical habitats, corridors, and potential of area for carbon sink. Overlays of socio-economic criteria, like poverty and ethnicity, will further help prioritise project areas within the candidate landscapes.

Implementation will be on a decentralised participatory approach with involvement of grass root level organisations in planning, decision making, implementation and monitoring. It will be implemented by the Gram Sabha and the Committees mandated by the Gram Sabha, including revamped JFMCs at village level, revamped Forest Development Agency (FDA) under the Chair of an elected representative at district/ division level, revamped State Forest Development Agency with a Steering Committee chaired by the Chief Secretary and an Executive Committee chaired by the Principal Chief conservator of Forests at the State/U.T. level. A Governing Council, chaired by the Minister, MoEF&CC and a National Executive Council chaired by the Secretary (EF&CC) and co-chaired by the Director General of Forests &Special Secretary with the Mission Director as the Member Secretary at the national level will facilitate Mission implementation. A multidisciplinary team, both from Government and Non Governmental Organisations (NGOs) will be mandated to facilitate planning and implementation at cluster/landscape unit level.

(c) Eco-mark Labeling Scheme in India

The MoEF&CC, Government of India, has launched the ecolabelling scheme known as "Ecomark" in to the market in 1991. India has made an eco-labelling scheme as a part of its environmental policy. The Ministry administers the programme with technical advice from the Central Pollution Control Board (CPCB). This scheme is linked to the product quality and safety standards of Bureau of Indian Standards (BIS). This scheme distinguishes itself from other international eco-labeling schemes, which are independent. Eco-mark has some product specific requirements that include clauses on energy conservation in the production process.

The "Eco-labels" represent a holistic view, giving an overall assessment of a product's impact on environment relative to other products in the same category. The criteria follow a cradle to grave approach - from raw material extraction, to manufacturing, and to disposal. Any product with the Ecomark will be the right environmental choice. "Eco-labeling" is a voluntary method of environmental performance certification and labeling that is practiced around the world. BIS, the national standards organisation of India, issues a certification mark to products conforming to a set of standards aimed at the least impact on the ecosystem. One of the purposes of the marking scheme is increasing awareness among the consumers towards reducing environment impact. The mark is issued to various product categories and the development of standards for more products is in progress. The description the CPCB has given for the logo speaks for itself. An earthen pot has been chosen as the logo for the Eco-mark scheme in India. The familiar earthen pot uses a renewable resource like earth, does not produce hazardous waste and consumes little energy in making. Its solid and graceful form represents both strength and fragility, which also characterises the eco-system.

The specific objectives of the scheme were as follows:-

(i) To provide an incentive for manufacturers and importers to reduce adverse environmental impact of products.

(ii) To reward genuine initiatives by companies to reduce adverse environmental impact of their products.

(iii) To assist consumers to become environmentally responsible in their daily lives by providing information to take account of environmental factors in their purchase decisions.

(iv) To encourage citizens to purchase products which have less harmful environmental impacts.

(v) Ultimately to improve the quality of the environment and to encourage the sustainable management of resources.

There will be three stages leading to the award of the "ECOMARK":-

(i) A Steering committee, set up in the MoEF&CC to determine the product categories for coverage under the scheme and also formulate strategies for promotion, implementation, future development and improvements in the working of the scheme.

(ii) A technical committee, set up in the CPCB, to identify the specific product to be selected and the individual criteria to be adopted, including, wherever possible, inter-se priority between the criteria if there be more than one.

(iii) The Bureau of Indian Standards to assess and certify the products and draw up a contract with the manufacturers, allowing the use of the label, on payment of a fee.

A steering Committee was set up in the MoEF&CC by the Central Government to decide the products categories to be taken up under the scheme, and to formulate the strategies for promotion, future development and improvement of this scheme. The product categories will be notified from time to time. The functions of the Steering Committee were as follows:-

(a) Selection of the logo for the "ECOMARK".

(b) Activities related to creation of mass awareness for promotion and acceptance of the scheme.

(c) Determining the product category to be taken up under the scheme.

(d) Co-ordinating ways of ensuring that industry is actively involved in the scheme.

(c) Securing the involvement of other Ministries, Government Departments, Industry Associations and other NGOs and Consumer organisations.

(f) Formulations of strategies for future development of the scheme.

(g) Identifying institutions in India or outside which are engaged in the standardisation of any article or process or improvement of quality of any article or process and recommending assistance to build consumer awareness.

(h) Promoting programmes of comparative testing of products by Consumer Organisations and dissemination their results to the general public.

(i) Supporting any research for the formulation of ECOMARK products in the interest of Consumer groups.

The composition of the Committee included Secretary, MoEF&CC as Chairman, and the other members are Secretary, Department of Civil Supplies (or his representative) Secretary, Ministry of Industry (or his representative), Secretary, Ministry of Chemicals and Petrochemicals (or his representative), Secretary, Ministry of Agriculture (or his representative), Secretary, Ministry of Information and Broad- casting (or his representative), Director General of Technical Development (or his representative), Director General, Council of Scientific and Industrial Research (or his representative), Director General, Health Services (or his representative), Development Commissioner, Small Scale Industries (or his representative),

Chairman, CPCB and not more than five non officials, to be nominated by the Central Government; to represent the interests of industry, consumer groups or other NGOs; of which at least two will represent Consumer groups. The officer in charge, "ECOMARK" in the MoEF&CC is its Member-Secretary. A Technical Committee was also constituted by the Central Government to identify the individual products and determine the criteria for awarding the ECOMARK. The Committee functions in the Central Pollution Control Board, Delhi.

The BIS was assigned the status of implementing the scheme. Its functions were (a) Assessing the product for Eco-mark, certify the product for award of the Eco-mark, (b) Review suspend or cancel a license, for the use of the Eco-mark; (c) Mark inspections, and take such samples for analysis of any material or substances as may be necessary to see whether any article or product in relation to which the Eco-mark has been used, conforms to the contract or whether the Eco-mark is improperly used in relation to any article or process with or without a license.

Under the scheme the manufacturers shall apply for testing and certification of products which fall under the notified categories in terms of their compliance with published environmental criteria in the prescribed form. The terms and conditions governing operations of licenses including fees shall be as per the Bureau of Indian Standards Act and the regulations framed there under. Testing and certification shall be carried out by the BIS. For product categories which have the Indian Standards mark, the BIS will ordinarily complete the task of certification within a period of three months. Products certified as eligible for the ECOMARK shall be licensed to carry the ECOMARK for a prescribed time period. The product shall be reassessed after the prescribed period and the license fee shall have to be paid again for the mark.

The criteria were for broad environmental levels and aspects, but will be specific at the product level. Products will be examined in terms of the following main environmental impacts:-

(a) That they have substantially less potential for pollution than other comparable products in production, usage and disposal.

(b) That they are recycled, recyclable, made from recycled products or biodegradable, where comparable products are not.

(c) That they make significant contribution to saving non-renewable resources, including non renewable energy sources and natural resources, compared with comparable products.

(d) That the product must contribute to a reduction of the adverse primary criteria which has the highest environmental impact associated with the use of the product, and which will be specifically set for each of the product categories.

The product general requirements deal with the issues of compliance of the pollution control acts; raising environmental awareness among consumers etc., in addition to safety, quality and performance of the products.

In determining the primary criteria for a product the following shall be taken (a) Production process including source of raw material; (b) Case of Natural Resources; (c) Likely impact on the environment; (d) Energy conservation in the production of the product; (e) Effect and extent of waste arising from the production process; (f) Disposal of the product and its container; (g) Utilisation of "Waste" and recycled materials; (h) Suitability for recycling or packaging (i) Biodegradability. The criteria were reviewed from time to time.

The label shall be awarded for a minimum period of one year and shall roll forward annually. The BIS has the power to withdraw the license at any time if they find any misleading information. The award may also be withdrawn in case of any change in criteria due to the advancement of technology or any other valid reasons, in consultation with the technical committee. The time period of the award was reviewed from time to time. The MoEF&CC took appropriate measures to launch a country wide mass awareness campaign, including encouraging consumer groups. Assistance was given to consumer organisations for comparative testing of products and dissemination of information to the public. As of now, the Government of India has notified the final criteria for around 16 product categories such as Soaps and Detergents, Paper, Food Items, Lubricating Oils, Packaging Materials, Architectural Paints and Powder Coatings, Batteries, Electrical/Electronic Goods, Food Additives, Wood Substitutes, Cosmetics, Aerosol Propellants, Plastic Products, Textiles, Fire-extinguisher and Leather.

Eco Labels available in India

- *Energy Efficiency Labeling:*

Energy labels are not proper eco labels because they focus on a single aspect and their use is often mandatory on certain products. STAR is a well-known environmental label focused on energy efficiency. It identifies and promotes energy-efficient products that have the same quality standards of equivalent models, and in addition reduce energy-related CO2 emissions and lead to cost savings.

The Bureau of Energy Efficiency (BEE), Ministry of Power has developed a scheme for energy efficiency labeling. The scheme was launched by the Hon'ble Minister of Power in May 2006 and is currently invoked for equipment/appliances (Frost Free (No-Frost) refrigerator, Tubular Fluorescent Lamps, Room Air Conditioners, Direct Cool Refrigerator, Distribution Transformer, Induction Motors, Pump Sets, Ceiling Fans, LPG, Electric Geysers, and Colour TV).

Under this program, for the benefit of general public, the appliance manufacturers could voluntarily affix BEE Star

Label on their appliances showing the level of energy consumption by the appliance both in terms of absolute values as well as equivalent number of stars varying from one to five, in accordance with specific stipulation. The greater the number of stars on the label, higher the appliance energy efficiency and lower its electricity consumption. However, from January 2010, affixing BEE star label has been made mandatory for Frost Free Refrigerators, whereas, BEE Labeling is still in the voluntary phase for Direct Cool Home Refrigerator.

- *Certification body for Sustainable Development*

An inspection and certification body for organic, fair trade, and good agricultural practices (GAP), named Ecocert, operates in eighty countries of the world. It provides inspection and certification services for safety of environment and mankind. In India, Ecocert operates from Aurangabad, Maharashtra. It covers South Asian countries. It has started its operations in India in 2002. Ecocert India has certified over three hundred thousand hectares of land for 170 of its clients constituting Processors, Exporters, Farmers' Groups and Individual Farmers. The main objective of Ecocert is to promote the India Organic logo in the international markets and the Agmark India Organic logo in the Indian markets and give recognition to organic produce from India. Regular audits by its Head Office and Accreditation agencies help Ecocert sustain the faith of the clients and consumers.

- *Forest Stewardship Council (FSC) Chain of Custody Certification*

FSC is a global, not-for-profit organisation devoted to the promotion of responsible forest management worldwide. It enables businesses and consumers to make informed choices about the forest products they buy, and create positive change by engaging the power of market dynamics. FSC certification is a voluntary, market-based system that allows companies to promote their products as deriving from well-managed forests. In India FSC is based in New Delhi. FSC facilitates the development of standards, ensures monitoring of certified operations and protects the FSC trademark so consumers can choose products that come from well-managed forest.

- Good Weave International

Good Weave International (GWI) is a non-governmental organisation working to end child labour in the handmade rug industry and offer educational opportunities to children in South Asia. The Good Weave certification program was formerly known as "RugMark". The Good Weave label is issued to rug manufacturers that adhere to the Generic Good Weave Standard, agree to its independent verification and voluntarily join as licensees. Good Weave's standard is currently being broadened to include additional labour and environmental criteria that aim to raise the standard of living in weaving communities and address the root causes of child labour. In India, Good Weave International is based in New Delhi and Varanasi. The organisation is not only concerned with eradicating child labour in the rug industry, but also working towards ensuring adult rug workers are treated fairly and that rugs made are not at the expense of their health, safety, or environment.

- *Green Globe Certification*

Green Globe is the global travel and tourism industries' certification program for sustainable tourism. Green Globe Members save energy and water resources, reduce operational costs, positively contribute to local communities and their environment and meet the high expectations of green leisure and business travelers. In India, there are accredited auditors who are professional environmental or sustainability consultants who have undergone Green Globe Certification training and are registered on an annual basis. Their role is to provide Green Globe clients with third party verification that certification criteria have been met. In India, there are tourist places like Svaastha Spa, Hotel United 21, Club Mahindra

Lakeview Munnar, and Club Mahindra Fort Kumbhalgarh have "Green Globe" label.

- *Organic Certification*

The Agricultural and Processed Food Products Export Development Authority (APEDA) is an export promotion organisation under Ministry of Commerce and Industries, Government of India. It is mandated with the responsibility of promotion and development of the export of its scheduled products. Indian National Standards for Organic Production and India Organic Logo is governed by APEDA, which provides national standards for organic products through a National Accreditation Policy and Programme. The aim of the National Programme for Organic Production (NPOP) is to provide the means of evaluation of certification programmes for organic agriculture and products as per internationally approved criteria and to accredit certification programmes. It also facilitates certification of organic products in conformity to the National Standards for Organic Products and encourages the development of organic farming and organic processing.

- *UPS Carbon Neutral*

The UPS Carbon Neutral shipping label indicates that UPS customers have offset the climate impact of the Green House Gases (GHG) emissions produced by the transportation of that shipment. UPS calculates the emissions and purchases carbon offset credits equivalent to the GHG emissions created in shipping the package to make it "carbon neutral". UPS has added India to its carbon neutral shipping programme. Under this programme, millions of customers now have the option to pay a small fee to calculate and offset the carbon emissions associated with their shipments. To use this service, users only need to check a box during the shipping process. UPS will calculate the carbon impact and purchase high quality certified carbon offsets on the customer's behalf. UPS targets offsets certified to the "Gold Standard," "Voluntary Carbon Standard" or "Climate Action Reserve."

- *The Green Signal*

Eco-label - The Green Signal - certifies environmental preferences adopted during the manufacturing of a product or a service. It is developed and certified by Ahmedabad based Indian Institute of Management. The Green Signal functions under the aegis of the Centre for Innovation, Incubation and Entrepreneurship (CIIE) at the Indian Institute of Management Ahmedabad (IIMA). The broader parameters for assessing a product or service are energy consumption, carbon footprints, water consumption, waste generation and management, and Corporate Social Responsibility (CSR) commitments of the entity.

- *ISO 14000*

The International Organisation for Standardisation (ISO) develops international standards for all industrial sectors. The ISO 14000 family addresses various aspects of environmental management. It provides practical tools for companies and organisations looking to identify and control their environmental impact and constantly improve their environmental performance. It is awarded to organisations that identify and control the environmental impacts, comply with environmental laws/regulations and fulfill other requirements and continually improve upon them.

- *Ecotel Certification*

The Ecotel certification is awarded to environmentally sensitive hotels. This certification recognises outstanding achievement along the triple bottom line: environmental, social, and fiscal parameters. It is based on five areas of environmental management - environmental commitment, solid waste management, energy efficiency, water conservation and employee environmental education and community involvement - each of the management area is designated by a globe award. To be certified the hotels must achieve at least two globe awards. The certification is valid for two years and hotels and restaurants seeking an upgrade or recertification must apply at the end of two years. Its India office based in Delhi conducts assignments within India and the Indian sub-continent for leading hotel companies, banks, and hotel development and investment groups.

- *Fair Trade*

Fair trade represents a new way to do business that looks holistically at the supply chain to address market failures and their social impact at source. It is not about aid or charity, but about recognizing the global community as having rights and responsibilities that extend across all of its stakeholders. Fair trade standards are designed to support the sustainable development of small producer organisations and agricultural workers in the poorest countries in the world. Its India office is based in Delhi and its mission is to be an organ of representation, coordination, exchange, and collabouration for the empowerment of small-scale farmers' and farm workers' organisations from Asia within the framework of Fair trade Certification.

- *Better Cotton Initiative*

A voluntary organisation, the Better Cotton Initiative (BCI) helps millions of farmer to grow cotton in a way that is good for the environment and the farmers and is more economical across the globe. It encourages farmers to adopt the better management practices in cultivation of cotton to achieve measurable reductions in main environmental impacts, while improving social and economic benefits for all cotton farmers across the world. The big challenges to making cotton more sustainable are excessive use of pesticides (bad for human health and the environment), environmentally inefficient production methods (which create water shortages and degrade the soil) and poor working conditions. Adidas, Gap Inc., H&M, ICCO, IFAP, IFC, IKEA, Organic Exchange, Oxfam, PAN UK, and WWF founded the Better Cotton Initiative in 2005 to take steps towards the sustainable and better management practices for the cultivation of cotton.

Better Cotton was first harvested from farmers in Brazil, India, Mali, and Pakistan in 2010-11. It is available 2012 onwards from China. Turkey is also aiming to produce Better Cotton as well. BCI for other regions is regularly in touch with organisations and governments to bring the Better Cotton programme.

- *Global Organic Textile Standards (GOTS)*

This is the leading textile processing standard for organic fibres worldwide, including ecological and social criteria, backed by independent certification of the entire textile supply chain. The aim to develop the Standards was to combine the various existing and draft standards in the area of eco textile processing. It defines the requirements to ensure the organic status of textiles- from harvesting of the raw material through responsible manufacturing of the product environmentally and socially to the labeling of the product. So it can provide a credible assurance to the end consumer. It covers the production, processing, manufacturing, packaging, labeling, exportation, importation and distribution of all natural fibres. Processors and manufacturers shall be enabled to supply their organic fabrics and garments with one certification accepted in all major selling markets. Version 3.0 was published on 1 March 2011, six years after the introduction of the initial version. High ecological and social requirements as well as global practicability and verifiability were taken into consideration in the revision work in order to achieve reliable and transparent criteria. The International Working Group is comprised of four reputed member organisations- the OTA (USA), IVN (Germany), Soil Association (UK) and JOCA (Japan), which contribute their respective expertise in organic farming and environmentally and socially responsible textile processing to GOTS together with other international stakeholder organisations and experts.

Popular Green Claims in India

Green claims that accurately convey the environmental attributes of products help consumers to make informed choices. Misleading, false, meaningless or unclear information can result in consumers losing confidence in environmental claims and labels in general, lead to unfair business competition and discourage companies from making truthful claims.

- *Mobius Loop*

The Mobius Loop is a universal recycling symbol. It is an internationally recognised symbol and often used to indicate that a product or its packaging is capable of recycling or has recycled content. It is composed of three mutually chasing arrows that form a Möbius strip (an unending single-sided looped surface). The inclusion of a number inside the loop shows the percentage of recycled material that has been used to make the product. But this claim is sustainable only if the local waste handling system accepts it.

- *Litter disposal symbol*

The presence of this symbol on products is often presumed to indicate its eco-friendliness. The symbol just encourages consumers to dispose waste responsibly.

- *Cruelty-free / Bunny logo*

This is a general claim that specifies that no animal testing have been done on the product and its ingredients. It is generally found on cosmetics and personal care products. However, the claim is not being verified by any government agency or any independent organisation. Most raw materials used in cosmetics were tested on animals years ago. The manufacturer might use those raw materials and base their 'cruelty-free' claim on the fact that the materials or products are not currently used on animals. The animal rights movement to describe products that have been manufactured without animal product often uses it.

Eco-mark Scheme- An analysis [CUTS Centre for International Trade, [Economics and Environment Research Report]

Eco-labels have three distinct dimensions attached to them. First, they are a part of the "sustainable consumption" agenda and aid consumers in making informed choices about the environmental impact of the products they consume. Second, they are a part of the "sustainable production" agenda: the products themselves, the processes by which they are manufactured, the usage to which they are subjected and the means of their disposal are certified to be environmentally superior to alternatives. Third, there appears a possibility that eco-labeling could be used as a protectionist measure, Non-Tariff Barrier (NTB) to international trade. Eco-labels have now become a part of the World Trade Organisation (WTO) agenda and are being discussed at the WTO in the Committee on Trade and Environment.

The effective implementation of any measure such as the Indian Eco-mark Scheme requires resources and political will. In case of the Eco-mark, there were both resources and political will when the Scheme was launched in the 1990s. However, with no political backup, the MoEF & CC has been unable to maintain the momentum and subsequently the Scheme has failed to acquire adequate support of the Ministry of Finance.

After a large amount of work and effort (e.g. on criteria development), the Government changed and the will to implement the Scheme was lost. Currently, the Indian Eco-mark Scheme has turned into a lame duck situation with lack of interest of most of the stakeholders. To a large extent, this is due to the lack of continuity of the concerned Governmental staff. A serious and complex issue such as eco-labeling must be handled by specialists who remain in the institution till the task is well accomplished.

Another reason behind the derailment of the Scheme was that some business lobbies worked hard to disrupt it: the detergent industry being a case in point. It must be realised that this is bound to happen initially, and that while voluntary adoption of the Scheme is highly advisable, the Government and civil society groups must show sufficient resolve by not allowing pressure groups to allow the Scheme to stand still.

Problems also exist in the administrative set up, as the implementation is in the hands of the BIS, which treats the Eco-mark Scheme somewhat like a step child. Communication between different branches/Ministries of the Government has been very poor at times, responsibilities have got diffused and the entire management has been weak. There is, therefore, a crying need to intensively re-examine the mechanics and modalities of managing and implementing the Scheme.

The Eco-mark Scheme has failed to take off in a desired fashion due to multiple reasons. Today, the multiplicity has made the situation so complex that it would be relatively easier to start from first principles, i.e. starting with a small basket of products/categories, which are the dirtiest ones so as to get a maximum impact. The past repository of knowledge could serve as a reference point.

It is further suggested that the MoEF&CC takes the initiative in reviving the Scheme. Given the resource constraints, this initiative would be a partnership between the Government, civil society organisations and industry. Within the Government, participation from the Ministry of Commerce and Industry, the Department of Consumer Affairs (DoCA) and the BIS and possibly other relevant Ministries such as Finance would be necessary but clearly, the MoEF&CC must take the lead role. The present Scheme needs to be restarted or even revitalised with a proactive and focused approach from the first principle with:

Eco-labeling Board: As the existing three-tier system has been too bureaucratic, a new, independent board with an advisory structure comprising of the scientific community, consumer, environmental and business groups would be a better option. Suitable promotional tools and techniques have to be devised to promote Eco-mark amongst individual consumers and institutional buyers.

Privatisation: There should be a reduction and prioritisation of the number of selected product categories to be included under the Scheme. Intermediate goods should continue to be considered under the Scheme. The product categories to be chosen should be based on certain measurable parameters such as maximum adverse environmental impact, and high national consumption. However, there should be a system that determines whether to include new product categories under the Scheme given the dynamics of the environment.

Forward Looking: The Scheme needs to be made more dynamic and forward looking by periodic revisions of criteria through wide stakeholder consultations. A system must be set in place that carries out the same every two years especially for rapidly changing technology products such as under the electronics product category. This will motivate and encourage industry to attain a higher gradation. Government should link such promotions with incentives in the form of excise duty exemption, rebates, preferential purchase or even tax holidays. In addition, the proposed criteria should also take into account existing Indian Standards that cover such product categories.

International Trade: As eco-labels can be used as NTBs, domestic as well as international requirements need to be balanced while formulating the criteria. The Government should press for equivalence and/or mutual recognition of the Schemes of different countries at the WTO, as it will prove beneficial for industries. Otherwise a situation may arise where companies having Indian Eco-mark certificate would need to apply for eco-label of the destination country, leading to dual cost. If getting an Indian Eco-mark would suffice for exporting the product to any country in the world, then an individual exporter would save substantially on certification costs and this, alone, would act as sufficient inducement for him to adopt the Eco-mark.

Awareness: Last but certainly not the least; an effective National Awareness Campaign should be carried out to raise both consumer and industrial awareness and demand for the

Eco-mark. The campaign should be carried out on a continuous basis to set in motion a market for green products.

(B) Ministry of Power

The Ministry of Power (MoP) came about in 1992, as the successor to the Ministry of Energy. Its primary responsibility is the development of electric power in India. The Ministry is responsible for the Administration of the Electricity Act, the Energy Conservation Act and to undertake development and enforcement tasks of these and other related acts.

Key legislation

The short and long term plans outlined above are just some of the many energy conservation initiatives taken up by the Ministry which impact green procurement. In order to achieve its targets, the MoP has also developed an increasingly well planned and diversified set of legislation and initiatives. The chief among these is the Energy Conservation Act from which are derived major initiatives like the BEE and the ECBC. Other key legislation as part of green initiatives overseen by the MoP include the Electricity Act, the NMEEE and the Standards and Labelling programme of the BEE. It is also responsible for further development, oversight and enforcement of these acts.

* *The Energy Conservation Act (ECA)*

Considering the vast potential of energy savings and benefits of energy efficiency, the Government of India enacted the Energy Conservation Act, 2001 (52 of 2001). The Act provides for the legal framework, institutional arrangement and a regulatory mechanism at the Central and State level to embark upon energy efficiency drive in the country. Five major provisions of EC Act relate to Designated Consumers, Standard and Labeling of Appliances, Energy Conservation Building Codes, Creation of Institutional Set up (BEE) and Establishment of Energy Conservation Fund.

The ECA became effective from 1st March, 2002 and BEE operationalised from 1st March, 2002. Energy efficiency institutional practices and programs in India are now mainly being guided through various voluntary and mandatory provisions of the ECA.

- *Energy Efficiency Measures*

(a) Standards and Labelling programme

Standards and labelling (S&L) programme has been identified as one of the key activities for energy efficiency improvements. A key objective of this scheme is to provide the consumer an informed choice about the energy saving and thereby the cost saving potential of the relevant marketed product. The scheme was launched by the Hon'ble Minister of Power on 18th May 2006 and is currently invoked for 12 equipments/appliances, i.e. Air Conditioners, Tube lights, Frost Free Refrigerators, Distribution Transformers, Induction Motors, Direct Cool Refrigerator, Geysers, Ceiling fans, Colour TVs, Agricultural pump sets, LPG stoves and Washing machine, of which the first 4 have been notified under mandatory labeling from 7th January, 2010. The other appliances are presently under voluntary labeling phase.

The energy efficiency labeling programs under BEE are intended to reduce the energy consumption of appliance without diminishing the services it provides to consumers. The scheme aims at providing information on energy performance of appliances based on the standards issued by BEE so that the consumers can make informed decisions while purchasing appliances. The STAR rating ranges from 1 to 5 in the increasing order of energy efficiency. In addition to the objective of informed choices to consumers, this program leads to huge energy savings and thereby the cost savings, reduces capital investment in energy supply infrastructure, enhances the product quality, strengthens the competitive markets, builds position for domestic industries to compete in such markets where norms for energy efficiency are mandatory, removes indirect barriers to trade, reduces carbon emission and helps meet climate change goals.

(b) Demand Side Management

The Demand Side Management and increased electricity end use efficiency can together mitigate power shortages to a certain extent and drastically reduce capital needs for power capacity expansion. The Bureau will be assisting 5 electric utilities to set up DSM Cell and will also assist in capacity building of DSM Cell staff. The preparation of investment grade feasibility reports on agricultural DSM, municipal water pumping and domestic lighting in each of the 5 states will also be undertaken by the Bureau under DSM programme.

(c) Energy Conservation Building Code (ECBC)

The Energy Conservation Building Code (ECBC) was launched by the Government of India on 27th May, 2007. The ECBC sets minimum energy standards for new commercial buildings having a connected load of 100kW or contract demand of 120kVA in terms of Energy Conservation (Amendment) Act, 2010. Harmonisation of ECBC with National Building Code (NBC) is also under progress by including a chapter on "Approach to Sustainability" in NBC 2005. BEE has developed Eco-Nirman conformance check tool with an objective of helping architects and design professionals to assess the conformance of their designs with code requirements.

Labeling programme for 3 categories of buildings (day use office buildings/BPOs/Shopping malls) has been developed and put in public domain. Till now 136 buildings have been found eligible for issue of label while ESCO model is being promoted for carrying out energy efficiency measures in existing buildings through performance contracting.

(d) Bachat Lamp Yojana (BLY)

Bachat Lamp Yojana (BLY) promotes energy efficient and high quality Compact fluorescent lamps (CFLs) as a replacement for incandescent bulbs in households at the rate of an incandescent bulb, i.e. ₹ 15. This would remove barrier of high CFL price (which is currently ₹ 80 - ₹ 100 per CFL) which is constraining its penetration into households. It targets replacement of about 400 million incandescent bulbs in use in the country, leading to a possible reduction of 4000 MW of electricity demand, and a reduction of about 24 million tonnes of CO_2 emissions every year. The price differential would be made up by project implementer through carbon credits earned which could be traded in the international market under Clean Development Mechanism (CDM) under the UNFCCC Kyoto protocol.

BEE has developed the umbrella framework BLY-Programme of Activities (PoA) which has been registered under UNFCCC-EB on 29th April, 2010. The PoA would define key CDM requirements, including the project baseline, additionality, methodology, monitoring protocols through which CO2 emission reductions would be assessed. The PoA approach reduces time and transaction costs for registering the projects since the key CDM requirements will not need to be addressed by area-specific projects within the PoA. BEE plays a role of a Coordinating and Managing Entity (CME) in the BLY - PoA. Kerala State has distributed the CFLs in the entire state. Karnataka State has also launched the scheme and CFL distribution has started. BLY is at different stages of implementation in many other states like Punjab, Haryana, Andhra Pradesh, Orissa, Chhattisgarh, Madhya Pradesh, Uttar Pradesh, Uttarakhand, Rajasthan, Goa, West Bengal, Tamilnadu and Delhi. These projects can be added to the registered umbrella framework as and when they are developed during the lifetime of the PoA.

(e) Strengthening Institutional Capacity of State Designated Agencies (SDAs)

State Designated Agencies (SDAs) are statutory bodies set up by states to implement energy conservation measures at state level. The main emphasis of the scheme is to build capacity of the SDAs to enable them to discharge regulatory, facilitative and enforcement functions under the ECA 2001. The scheme seeks to develop and implement Energy Conservation Action Plan (ECAP) based on a uniform template evolved for taking measures necessary to build institutional and human capacity, enabling the SDAs to implement energy efficiency programmes and undertake evaluation and monitoring of the Energy conservation activities implemented in the state. Till date, 32 States/UTs have designated their SDAs to coordinate, regulate and enforce the provisions of ECA, 2001.

Most of these organisations have limited experience in energy efficiency / conservation. This resulted in the need for building capacity, enhancing their understanding and knowledge about energy efficiency, having a common action plan to implement measures to reduce energy intensity of the State etc. The approved scheme of the Ministry of Power therefore enables SDAs to:

- Prepare a 5 year Energy Conservation Action Plan (ECAP)
- Implementation of ECAP with yearly deliverables
- Enhance capacity to undertake regulatory duties that they are required to perform under the Act.

The Ministry of Power had approved the scheme to provide financial support to the SDAs for strengthening their institutional capacity. Under the SDA scheme, financial support was provided to the SDAs to carry out the following activities:

- Creation of IT infrastructure
- Creation of database for Energy Managers / Energy Auditors and Designated Consumers and other stakeholders.

- Organizing workshops / training programmes
- Creating awareness through electronic media / print media
- Preparation of Detailed Project Reports of Govt. Buildings under IGEA.
- Implementation of Energy Efficiency Demonstration Projects in the area of energy efficient street lighting, revamping of drinking water pumping system and energy efficiency in SMEs clusters
- To convert the existing incandescent bulbs (ILBs) in the households and the street lights of one village with LEDs.

(f) State Energy Conservation Fund (SECF)

SECF is a statutory requirement under section 16 of the Energy Conservation Act 2001 and is one of the key elements of the ECAP. The scheme is for support of ₹ 70 crore as contribution by BEE to SECF to invest in Energy Efficiency projects. The effort will be to create a pool of financially sustainable activities for SDAs (like training programmes, fee for services, etc) which can augment the fund. The Ministry of Power has approved the scheme "Contribution to SECF by the Bureau of Energy Efficiency" for which ₹ 70 crore was sanctioned and to be disbursed during the last three financial years of the XI five year plan, i.e. 2009-10, 2010-11 and 2011-12. The funds were disbursed to those states that have constituted their state energy conservation fund and finalised the rules and regulations to operationalise the same.

(g) Energy Efficiency in Small and Medium Enterprises (SMEs) and Designated Consumers

Energy use and technology gap study has been completed in 20 SMEs cluster and is in progress in other 5 clusters. Cluster specific manual on energy conservation opportunities have been prepared in 20 clusters and information dissemination workshop for various stakeholders have been completed in 34 clusters. Preparation of DPRs on energy efficient technologies in under progress and peer review of the prepared DPRs is being done by SIDBI. Capacity building workshop for Local Service Providers (LSPs) has been organised in 4 clusters. BEE also initiated the Small Group Activities (SGA) and Total Energy Management (TEM) programme to inculcate the energy efficiency practices in SMEs with support of experts from Japan. The pilot activities of SGA/TEM have been implemented in three SMEs clusters (9 units) so far.

(h) Professional Certification and Accreditation

As per the Energy Conservation Act, it is mandatory for all the designated energy consumers to get energy audit conducted by an Accredited Energy Auditor and to designate or appoint an Energy Manager. The Government of India has specified the passing of the National level certification examination as the qualification for a Certified Energy Manager and Certified Energy Auditor. BEE has taken up the challenge of creating a cadre of professionally qualified energy managers with expertise in energy management, project management, financing and implementation of energy efficiency projects, and policy analysis.

The Bureau has successfully conducted Ten National Certification Examinations since 2004. After 10th Examination, 8026 persons have been qualified as energy managers out of which 5731 have been qualified as energy auditors. The Guide Books for the Energy Managers and Energy Auditors have been revised. The 11th Examination for the fresh candidates has been held on 5th and 6th February, 2011 based on the revised syllabus. The capacity building of energy managers and energy auditors through National Certification Examination route will have a long-term impact on the Indian economy by making it less energy intensive.

The Central Government, vide Notification of 12th March, 2007, has notified 9 energy intensive industries as designated consumers. The Bureau of Energy Efficiency (Qualification of Accredited Energy Auditors and Maintenance of their List)

Regulations, 2010 has also been notified on 31st March 2010. The above Regulation lays down the procedures for constitution of Accreditation Advisory Committee and qualifications for accredited energy auditor. The accreditation process is proposed to be completed twice in a year by the Accreditation Advisory Committee, constituted by the Bureau.

(i) Manual and Codes

Energy audits have been conducted in past with little or no standard test procedures and inadequate instrumentation. When Manuals of standardised test procedures are available and uniform codes are adopted, there would be increased awareness and clarity among users regarding the output from an energy audit. Manuals and codes on 7 Technologies (Equipment) Lighting Systems; Dryers; Cogeneration Plants; Electric Motors; Electric Transformers; Fluid piping systems (network), insulation and Air Conditioners/Chillers (HVAC) have been prepared. The manuals and code would help in standardizing the process of energy audit to support energy manager and energy auditors.

(j) School Education Programme

Considering the need to make the next generation more aware regarding efficient use of energy resources, it is necessary to introduce children during their school education. In this regard, promotion of energy efficiency in schools is being promoted through the BEACON project which is now in its third phase. The main methodology being adopted by this project is to train a minimum of 3 teachers as Master Trainers from 30 schools across several towns and cities in 22 states. These master trainers will assume the role of further training other teachers and students to ensure sustainability and continuity of the project.

Through this project recommendations will also be made to the National Council of Education, Research and Training

(NCERT) to update the science text books of classes VII to IX to include relevant chapters on Energy Efficiency in the school syllabus.

(k) Indo-German Energy Efficiency Project (Phase-Ii)

The Phase-I of the Indo-German Energy Efficiency Project has been successfully completed by the Bureau of Energy Efficiency (BEE) in September 2009. Activities in the Phase-II of the Project have already begun and the project would be supporting the thrust areas of the Bureau as mentioned above.

(l) Energy Conservation Awards

The Energy Conservation Awards recognise innovation and achievements in energy conservation by the Industries, buildings, zonal railways, state designated agencies, aviation; manufacturers of BEE star labeled appliances and municipalities and raise awareness that energy conservation plays a big part in India's response to reducing global warming through energy savings.

These examples suggest the potential for large scale replication, and of concrete measures which can help mitigate global warming. The awards scheme has been in operation since 1991. 32 sectors of Industry and other establishments are included in the Awards. In the Awards 2010, a new category for Thermal Power Stations has also been introduced so as to recognise their initiatives and efforts undertaken to conserve energy.

The responses among the industrial and commercial units have become very encouraging as is evident from the increasing participation level (from 123 in 1999 to 592 in 2010). The participating units of 2010 awards have collectively invested ₹ 5457 crore in energy conservation measures, and achieved a monetary savings of ₹ 2138 crore every year, implying a payback period of 31 months only, once again proving the fact that energy conservation is a least cost option. The participating units have also saved electrical energy of 2422 Million kWh of electrical energy, which is equivalent to the energy generated form a 357 MW thermal power station at a PLF of 0.775. In other words, these participating units have avoided the installation of power generating capacity equivalent to 357 MW thermal power stations in 2009-10, which would otherwise have been required to meet the power demand of these units.

In the last 12 years of Award Scheme of the period 1999-2010, the participating units have collectively saved ₹ 13399 crore and the investment made on energy efficiency projects was recovered back in 20 months. In energy terms, 14535 Million kWh of electrical power, 27 lakhs kilolitre of oil, 91 lakhs metric tonne of coal and 22 billion cubic metre of gas was saved, through the energy conservation measures of the participating units.

Speaking on the occasion, the then Union Power Minister, Shri Sushil Kumar Shinde said, "Energy conservation across all sectors of the economy is essential for balancing growth in energy demand and economic growth, while ensuring that India's access to energy is managed efficiently. India is one of the first developing countries to have achieved the unique distinction of successfully achieving the decoupling of economic growth from energy use. The National Energy Conservation Awards are a testament to the Government's and the industry's commitment towards efficient energy management and conservation."

In his address, Shri P. Uma Shankar, the then Secretary (Power), said, "The Energy Conservation Awards have motivated the participating units to undertake serious efforts in saving energy and safeguarding the environment." It is hoped that National Energy Conservation Award Scheme would help in motivating the other energy consumers in joining and promotion of a nationwide energy conservation movement.

(m) Painting Competition on Energy Conservation, 2010

Ministry of Power has undertaken National Campaign on Energy Conservation 2010. Under this campaign, a painting competition on energy conservation at School, State and National level are conducted. The painting competition is first conducted at the School level and two best paintings from the participating school are included in the concerned State/UT level Competition. First two winners from each State and UTs are invited to participate at the national level competition. Around 47155 Schools and 15.63 lakhs students of 4th, 5th and 6th standards of the 35 States and Union Territories participates in the School Level Painting Competition, which was quite encouraging. This competition is aimed at motivating the children towards energy conservation and offers them a chance to explore their creativity. The expressive paintings of the children reflected their interest in the energy conservation activities and their concern about climate change.

(n) National Mission for Enhanced Energy Efficiency (NMEEE)

The National Mission for Enhanced Energy Efficiency is one of the eight missions under the National Action Plan on Climate Change. The scheme has been approved by the cabinet and its implementation is under process. The objective of the Mission is to achieve growth with ecological sustainability by devising cost effective strategies for end-use demand side management. The Ministry of Power (MoP) and Bureau of Energy Efficiency (BEE) have been entrusted with the task of preparing the implementation plan for the NMEEE and to upscale the efforts to create and sustain market for energy efficiency to unlock investment of around ₹ 74,000 crore. The Mission, by 2014-15, is likely to achieve about 23 million tons oil-equivalent of fuel savings- in coal, gas, and petroleum products, along with an expected avoided capacity addition of over 19,000 MW. The carbon dioxide emission reduction is estimated to be 98.55 million tons annually. NMEEE will usher in the following four initiatives, in addition to the policies and programmes for energy efficiency being implemented by BEE. These initiatives are as follows:

- Perform Achieve and Trade (PAT), which is a market, based mechanism to enhance cost effectiveness of improvements in energy efficiency in energy-intensive large industries and facilities, through certification of energy savings that could be traded.

Targets for improvements in energy efficiency will be set under Section 14 of the Energy Conservation Act, 2001 in a manner that reflects fuel usage and the economic effort involved. The Government, in March 2007, notified units in nine sectors, namely aluminium, cement, chlor-alkali, fertilisers, iron and steel, pulp and paper, railways, textiles and thermal power plants, as Designated Consumers (DCs).

Designated Consumers (DCs) in 8 industrial sectors will have mandatory participation in the 1st cycle of PAT scheme which is being implemented during 2011-12 to 2013-14. It is estimated that the total energy consumption by about 462 DCs in 8 energy intensive sector is about 165 million tons of oil equivalent (MTOE) with Power Plant sector having the lion's share (i.e. 64 per cent). Moreover, only 5 sectors like Power plant, Iron and Steel, Cement, Fertiliser and Aluminum do consume 97 per cent of total energy consumed by 8 sectors. About 5.4 per cent reductions which are estimated at 8.97 MTOE are targeted in 3 years from energy intensive industries. Among the 23 MTOE set as target from NMEEE, implementation of PAT scheme do focus on achieving 8.97 MTOE by the end of first PAT cycle.

In an effort to provide an online platform to operationalise the PAT scheme, development of an internet based system (PATNET) is under process and work-order on PATNET has been awarded to NIIT to develop the e-platform of entire PAT scheme.

- Market Transformation for Energy Efficiency (MTEE) to accelerate the shift to energy efficient appliances in designated sectors through innovative measures to make the products more affordable with focus on leveraging international financial instruments, including Clean Development Mechanism (CDM) to make energy efficient appliances affordable and increase their levels of penetration.

Since the public sector holds the key to aggregation of CDM projects so as to reduce transaction costs, barriers to widespread adoption of CDM need to be removed through the following measures.

- Make it mandatory for all public investment and over time, all public operations to be assessed for their potential to attract carbon finance
- Promote programmatic CDM to reduce transaction costs and aggregation of small energy-efficiency projects
- Develop and implement a national CDM strategy for energy efficiency
- Promote market access of small industries in energy-efficiency projects
- Promote transparency in pricing
- Ensure that the legal status of CERs is clear to avoid disputes related to taxation
- Enhance capacity-building and training

The PoA would define key CDM requirements, including the project baseline, additionality, methodology, monitoring protocols through which CO2 emission reductions would be assessed. The PoA approach reduces time and transaction costs for registering the projects since the key CDM requirements will not need to be addressed by area-specific projects within the PoA. BEE plays a role of a coordinating and managing entity (CME) in the BLY - PoA which has already been explained in the previous sections.

Another program under this initiative is the development of Super Efficient Equipment Programme (SEEP). This program is proposed to develop superefficient appliances with an aim to reduce consumption and enable demand side management. The goal is not only to reduce cost of energy efficient equipments to stimulate accelerated market transformation but also to encourage domestic manufacturing to sustain the market.

- Energy Efficiency Financing Platform (EEFP), to help stimulate necessary funding for Energy Service Company (ESCO) based delivery mechanisms for energy efficiency. The costs will be recovered from the energy savings, which will also reduce the subsidy bill of the state government. The scheme has the potential to be replicated across the country. BEE has undertaken the following measures, in addition to those related to implementing demonstration projects in government buildings, in order to stimulate the market.

- Putting in place a government-supported standard methodology that covers the entire project chain from audit to performance measurement and verification
- Designing a standard performance contract
- Designing appropriate financial mechanisms to fund projects
- Implementing projects and evaluating their impact
- Building capacity in ESCOs and project owners

In an effort to provide EEFP, MoUs with M/s. PTC India Ltd, M/s. SIDBI and HSBC Bank have been signed by BEE. PTC India Ltd. has commenced financing of several building energy efficiency projects in Rashtrapati Bhavan Estate, ESIC Hospitals at Rohini and East Delhi, AIIMS, Safdarjung Hospital. SIDBI has taken up project preparation of energy efficiency projects in 25 SME clusters which will then be offered financing. Further, investment grade energy audits have been completed for large public buildings in the country. Based on the recommendations of these audits iconic buildings in the states will be taken up for implementation through Energy Service Companies (ESCO) route.

- Framework for Energy Efficient Economic Development (FEEED), seeks to develop fiscal instruments to promote energy efficiency including innovative fiscal instruments and policy measures like the Partial Risk Guarantee Fund (PRGF) and Venture Capital Fund for Energy Efficiency (VCFEE), Public Procurement of energy efficient goods and services, Utility based Demand Side Management (DSM), etc. Efforts of the government to create a market for energy efficiency need to be supplemented with appropriate fiscal instruments, which must be designed to address the following objectives:

  - Reassuring lenders by providing a guarantee for performance contracts
  - Providing a venture capital fund from the Government to provide equity for energy-efficiency projects
  - Promoting leadership in the public sector on energy efficiency
  - Promoting energy efficiency in public procurement based on life cycle cost analysis
  - Promoting regulatory incentives to state utilities through electricity regulatory commissions for DSM projects
  - Offering concessions on taxes and duties to attract investment

- *Partial Risk Guarantee Fund (PRGF)*

A PRGF is a risk sharing mechanism lowering the risk to the lender by substituting part of the risk of the borrower by granting guarantees ensuring repayment of part of the loan upon a default event. The guarantee can seek to directly support financing of energy-efficiency projects by:

- Addressing credit risk and barriers to structuring the transactions involved in financing energy-efficiency projects and

- Engaging commercial financial institutions and building their capacity to finance energy-efficiency projects on a commercially sustainable basis.
- *Venture Capital Fund for Energy Efficiency (VCFEE)*

VCFEE as envisaged by the Government of India under the National Mission for Enhanced Energy Efficiency can go long way in addressing the barriers and kick starting some of the long awaited energy efficiency projects in the country. This fund will work with following criteria:

- It is a Fund providing risk capital support to energy efficiency investments in new technology, goods and services, etc
- It is a leveraging fund with a view to leverage private venture investments in energy efficiency sector by identifying the possible co-investment opportunities (not in competition with other private funds) with other venture capitalists into Energy Efficiency projects and companies.
- It allows private venture fund players to capitalise the transaction costs associated with specific EE investments
- It helps to create the volume in energy efficiency deal flow by the fund manager of VCFEE through advertising and soliciting opportunities in energy efficiency area.
- In investments, where it co-invests with other venture capitalist on same return expectation as private venture capitalist, this Fund could be last to be paid in case of liquidation of investment in projects
- In investment, where it co-invests with other venture capitalist on lesser return expectation than private venture capitalist, this Fund then should be the first paid in case of liquidation of investment.

Under this initiative, framework development for financial institutions to promote energy efficiency is in process. Document on institutional framework and RFP for hiring fund manager for Partial Risk Guarantee Fund (PRGF) and Venture Capital Fund (VCF) are being finalised. Study on fiscal and monetary policy of energy efficiency projects have been awarded to National Institute of Public Finance and Policy (NIPFP).

(C) Ministry of New and Renewable Energy

The Ministry of New and Renewable Energy (MNRE) is the nodal Ministry of the Government of India for all matters relating to new and renewable energy. The broad aim of the Ministry is to develop and deploy new and renewable energy for supplementing the energy requirements of the country. The role of new and renewable energy has been assuming increasing significance in recent times with the growing concern for the country's energy security.

Energy self-sufficiency was identified as the major driver for new and renewable energy in the country in the wake of the two oil shocks of the 1970s. The sudden increase in the price of oil, uncertainties associated with its supply and the adverse impact on the balance of payments position led to the establishment of the Commission for Additional Sources of Energy in the Department of Science and Technology in March 1981. The Commission was charged with the responsibility of formulating policies and their implementation, programmes for development of new and renewable energy apart from coordinating and intensifying R&D in the sector. In 1982, a new department, i.e., Department of Non-conventional Energy Sources (DNES), that incorporated CASE, was created in the then Ministry of Energy. In 1992, DNES became the Ministry of Non-conventional Energy Sources. In October 2006, the Ministry was re-christened as the Ministry of New and Renewable Energy.

Key legislation

Renewable energy has been an important component of India's energy planning process since quite some time. MNRE is the nodal Ministry of the Government of India at the Federal level for all matters relating to new and renewable energy. The Ministry has been facilitating the implementation of broad spectrum programmes including harnessing renewable power, renewable energy to rural areas for lighting, cooking and motive power, use of renewable energy in urban, industrial and commercial applications and development of alternate fuels and applications. In addition, it supports research, design and development of new and renewable energy technologies, products and services. The Ministry either oversees or is involved with most energy legislation in the country, ranging from the NMEEE to the ECA. It is also responsible for administering the National Solar Mission and development and enforcement of the country's renewable energy targets through the NAPCC. The Ministry is also involved in allocation of subsidies, development of the Taxable Trading Certificate Scheme as well as supporting Programmes like those for information and public awareness as per the Tenth and Eleventh Five year plans.

(D) Ministry of Commerce and Industry (Department of Commerce)

The mandate of the Department of Commerce (DoC) is regulation, development and promotion of India's international trade and commerce through formulation of appropriate international trade and commercial policy and implementation of the various provisions thereof. The basic role of the Department is to facilitate the creation of an enabling environment and infrastructure for accelerated growth of international trade.

Key legislation

Until the 11th Plan, the DoC had little involvement in green procurement legislation in India. However, the introduction of the NAPCC and other initiatives within the 11th Plan has changed this scenario. There is an increasing level of cooperation and input from the DoC with the MNRE, MoEF&CC and the MoP to push through green initiatives in the country. Initial steps have been taken like the lowering of tariffs of certain battery components of electric vehicles and sustainable products.

(E) Bureau of Energy Efficiency

The BEE was established in 2002 under the provisions of the Energy Conservation Act, 2001. The mission of the Bureau of Energy Efficiency is to assist in developing policies and strategies with a thrust on self-regulation and market principles, within the overall framework of the ECA with the Primary objective of reducing energy intensity of the Indian economy. The role of BEE has already been explained in the previous sections.

Key legislation

The key pieces of legislation and initiatives that the Bureau is involved with are the ECA, the Electricity Act, NMEEE and the Standards and Labelling initiative which has already been explained. The latter is one which falls almost completely under the purview of the BEE, unlike the other acts listed.

(F) Central Pollution Control Board (CPCB)

The CPCB, a statutory Organisation, was constituted in 1974 under the Water (Prevention and Control of Pollution) Act. Further, it was entrusted with the powers and functions under the Air (Prevention and Control of Pollution) Act in 1981. It serves as a field formation and also provides technical services to the MoEF&CC of the provisions of the EPA.

Key legislation

The major legislation that falls under the CPCB which effects green initiative is the emission norms for motor vehicles. The Bharat emission norms were designed to be equivalent to the current Euro norms and are applicable to all vehicles using fossil fuels across the country. The CPCB is also involved in the Ecomark scheme and in the drafting of the new E-waste rules of 2010 and 2013 and will have a hand in the further development and implementation of the same. It also handles environmental zoning and planning along with the MoEF & CC.

(G) Bureau of Indian Standards

The BIS is the national standards organisation of India under the aegis of Ministry of Consumer Affairs, Food & Public Distribution, Government of India. It was founded in 1987, replacing the Indian Standards Institute.

Key legislation

The BIS, along with the MoEF&CC and the CPCB administers and implements the Ecomark scheme in India. Due to the requirement of quality labeling on any Eco-mark product, the BIS administers to both.

CHAPTER -3

SUSTAINABLE DEVELOPMENT IN INDIA

SUSTAINABLE DEVELOPMENT:-THEORETICAL EXPLANATION

(a) Economy-Environment Linkages

Economic activities either affect or are affected by natural and environmental resources. Economic activities such as extraction, processing, manufacture, transport, consumption and disposal, change the stock of natural resources, add stress to environmental systems and introduce wastes to environmental media. Moreover, present economic activities affect the stock of natural resources available for the future and have inter-temporal welfare effects. As a result, the productivity of an economic system depends in part on both supply and quality of natural and environmental resources. Thus, economic management impacts on the environment and environmental quality impacts on efficient working of the economy. Environmental degradation imposes costs on the economy which results in output and human capital losses.

(b) Definition of Sustainable Development and its explanation.

The term Sustainable Development rose to significance after the World Commission on Environment and

Development in its 1987 seminal report called "Our Common Future". Brundtland Commission defines Sustainable Development as "Development that meets the needs of the present generation without compromising the ability of future generations to meet their own needs".

This definition contains three concepts that require explanation. They are: needs, development and future generation. The use of the concept "needs" in the definition, is linked to the distribution of resources. It also in particular refers to the essential needs of the world's poor, to which overriding priority should be given. Development on the other hand is a qualitative concept incorporating notions of improvement and progress and including culture, social and economic dimensions. In more specific terms Sustainable Development aims at reducing the absolute poverty of the world's poor by providing lasting and secure livelihoods that minimise resource depletion, environmental degradation, cultural disruption and social instability.

(c) Components of Sustainability

There are three basic components of sustainable development; economic, social and the environment component. The three components are interdependent. The economic component of the concept consists of optimizing the use of limited resources and the management of material and energy saving technologies. Such management would create a stream of cumulative income, which would preserve -and not reduce - the cumulative capital (physical, natural and human) employed in the creation of this cumulative income. At the same time, the transition to an information society results in the change of the cumulative capital structure to favour human, increasing non-material streams of finance, information and intellectual property. By this time, these streams exceed seven times the volume of movement in material goods.

The social component is oriented to human development, preserved stability of public and cultural systems, and the reduction of the amount of societal conflict. The human being should not be viewed as an object, but rather the subject of development. He or she should take part in the formation of their own life, making and executing decisions, and exercising control over their implementation. An important part in creating these conditions belongs to the fair distribution of benefits amongst people (the reduction of the so-called GINI-index), the pluralism of opinions and tolerance for relations between people, the preservation of cultural capital and its varieties, first of all, of the heritage of non-dominating cultures.

From an ecological perspective, sustainable development provides for the integrity of both natural biological and physical systems and ensures their viability. The global stability of the biosphere depends upon it. Special significance is attached to the ability of such systems to self reproduce and adapt to various changes, as opposed to being preserved in a static condition within a vacuum or deteriorating and losing its biological variety.

(d) Rules of Sustainable Development

The basic implication of the concept of sustainable development that one may comprehend from definition involving inter generational equity is that, we should leave to the next generation a stock of 'quality of lift' assets no less than those we have inherited. This can be interpreted to mean:

a. That the next generation should inherit such a stock of wealth, comprising man-made assets and environmental assets.

b. That the next generation should inherit stock environmental assets no less than that inherited by the previous generation.

c. That the components of the inherited stock should be man made assets, natural assets and human assets.

The first interpretation stresses all capital assets: man made and natural. The second emphasises on natural capital only and the third includes human capital besides natural and man made capital. Based on the classification of capital, sustainability of development process may be verified. The dilemma or conflict here is whether sustainability rule should be defined in terms of natural capital alone or in terms of aggregate capital stock, where aggregate capital stock includes.

a. Man made capital (KMc) consisting of machines, building, roads etc.

b. Human capital (KHc) comprising of the stock of knowledge and skills.

c. Natural capital (KNc) that include all renewal and non renewable resources or any natural asset yielding a flow of ecological services with economic values over time.

There are two variants of this rule, a weak sustainability rule that requires that the total capital stock - physical, human and natural - are non declining through time and strong sustainability rule that requires that the nations stock of natural capital is non declining. Weak sustainability rule implies that we can pass on fewer environments so long as we offset this loss by increasing the stock of roads and machinery or other man made physical capital. Weak sustainability rule will hold if there is perfect substitutability between different forms of capital.

(e) Realizing Sustainable Development

The basic principles of sustainable development make it possible to harmonise the various sectoral and development strategies with the horizontal strategy on sustainable development (hereinafter: Strategy) and they also provide a general type of guidance for determining the Strategy's priorities, more specifically defined goals and tasks, the frameworks and means of implementation, in a coordinated and harmonised way. The basic principles have been formulated, clarified, and adopted at the highest levels by the relevant bodies of both the United Nations (UN) and the European Union (EU). On account of their national relevance the following should be highlighted from the complete set of principles:

- The principle of holistic approach: - Things must be viewed as a system of inter-related elements, the elements themselves also being systems interacting with one another. Any intervention may trigger ripple effects even in remote systems. So local challenges can be adequately addressed relying on the knowledge of the wider environment and global trends alike.
- Principle of intra-generational and inter-generational solidarity: - The interests of sustainable development are focused on people. The development and environmental needs of present generations must be addressed without compromising the ability of future generations to meet their own needs.
- The principle of social justice: - The right to adequate conditions for living must be recognised and fundamental human rights must be guaranteed for all. All people should have equal opportunities for acquiring knowledge and skills required to become worthy members of society.
- The principle of sustainable management of resources:- Sustainable management of resources with a view to the limitations of the carrying capacity of the environment; by using natural resources in a prudent and thrifty way it preserves resources required for future development. Biodiversity is also a natural resource and we attach high priority to its conservation.
- The principle of integration: - In the course of elaborating, evaluating, and implementing sectoral policies, plans, and programmes; economic, social, and environmental considerations and their relationships must also be taken into account to ensure that they can mutually reinforce each other. Local, regional, and national activities must be coordinated.

- The principle of utilizing local resources: - Efforts should be made to supply the needs of communities on a local level, from local resources. Local features and diversity should be preserved. Preservation and sustainable utilisation of the man-made environment and cultural heritage are also very important tasks.
- The principle of public participation: - Adequate access to information affecting social/economic life and the environment, to information on decision making processes must be provided for all. People's knowledge about sustainable development, its social/economic and environmental implications, and about sustainable solutions and approaches must be clarified and enhanced. Public participation in decision making should be strengthened.
- The principle of social responsibility: - To enable sustainable development and to make a higher quality of life possible; unsustainable patterns of production and consumption must be changed. Businesses' social responsibility must be strengthened, along with cooperation between the private and the public sector.
- The principle of precaution and prevention: - The precautionary approach means that wherever the possibility of severe or irreversible damage is perceived, a lack of complete scientific certainty may not be used as an excuse for delaying effective action to prevent damage to the environment or endangering human health; i.e. action must be taken in view of the gravity of the perceived threat. Human activities must be planned and carried out in line with this precautionary principle and activities damaging or polluting the environment endangering natural systems and human health must be prevented and - where it is not possible - reduced, and finally, damages must be restored to their original state as far as possible.
- The polluter pays principle: - Prices must reflect the real costs paid by society for activities involved in consumption and production as well as for their impacts, including the costs of using natural resources. Those engaged in activities damaging/polluting the environment must pay for damage caused to human health or the environment.

University of Maryland School of Public Policy professor and former Chief Economist for the World Bank Herman E. Daly (working from theory initially developed by Romanian economist Nicholas Georgescu-Roegen and laid out in his 1971 opus "The Entropy Law and the Economic Process") suggests the following operational rules defining the condition of ecological (thermodynamic) sustainability:. The principles are as follows:-

The main principle, he says, is to limit the human scale to a level which is within the carrying capacity of the environment. The carrying capacity of the environment is like a 'plimsoll line' of the ship which is the load limits mark for the ship.

Secondly, technological progress should be throughout efficiency increasing rather that throughput quantity increasing.

Thirdly, renewable resources should be exploited on a profit maximizing sustainable yield basis and in general not be driven to extinction, i.e., harvesting rate should not exceed regeneration rate.

Fourthly, for non renewable, rate of depletion should not exceed rate of creation of renewable substitutes, Besides these market failure related to resource pricing and property rights should be corrected.

Some commentators have argued that the "Daly Rules," being based on ecological theory and the Laws of Thermodynamics, should perhaps be considered implicit or foundational for the many other systems that are advocated, and are thus the most straightforward system for operationalisation of the Bruntland Definition. In this view, the Bruntland Definition and the Daly Rules can be seen as complementary. Bruntland provides the ethical goal of non-depletion of natural capital, Daly details parsimoniously how this ethic is operationalised in physical terms. The system is rationally complete, and in agreement with physical laws. Other definitions may thus be superfluous, or mere glosses on the immutable thermodynamic reality.

(II) India and Sustainable Development

(a) Ministry of Environment, Forest and Climate Change (MoEF&CC's) vision towards Sustainable Development.

The MoEF&CC is the nodal agency in the administrative structure of the Central Government, for planning, promotion, co-ordination and overseeing the implementation of environmental, forestry and wildlife programmes and policies. While implementing these policies and programmes, the Ministry is guided by the principle of sustainable development and enhancement of human well-being. The Ministry also serves as the nodal agency in the country for the United Nations Environment Programme (UNEP), South Asia Co-operative Environment Programme (SACEP), and International Centre for Integrated Mountain Development (ICIMOD) as well as for follow-up on the United Nations Conference on Environment and Development (UNCED). The Ministry is also entrusted with issues relating to multilateral bodies such as the Commission on Sustainable Development (CSD), Global Environment Facility (GEF) and of regional bodies like Economic and Social Council for Asia and Pacific (ESCAP) and South Asian Association for Regional Cooperation (SAARC) on matters pertaining to environment.

Its main activities include conservation and survey of natural resources including flora, fauna, forests, wildlife, aquatic bodies and water resources, and eco-systems, prevention and control of pollution and management of hazardous substances, protection of the environment and forests, including their biodiversity, mitigation and adaptation to climate change through measures that include afforestation, regeneration of degraded areas, and adoption of cleaner technologies, and promoting sustainable development and better environmental governance while protecting human, plant and animal life, health and welfare.

The main tools used to discharge its function of Sustainable Development include, inter alia, conducting surveys; collecting, compiling and disseminating data and information; undertaking scientific research, extension services and analyses; carrying out impact assessment of developmental projects and programmes; regulating use of natural resources; undertaking regeneration programmes; providing technical, scientific, financial and administrative support to organisations and institutions; imparting education, training, building capacity and generating awareness among stakeholders and the public at large; and promoting international cooperation through bilateral, regional and multilateral initiatives in environment and ecology.

(b) Vision of the Ministry for the Twelfth Plan towards realisation of Sustainable Development.

In the Twelfth Five Year Plan, the vision for this Ministry has been stated as "Managing Environment, Forests, Wildlife and challenges due to Climate Change for faster and equitable growth, where ecological security for sustainability and inclusiveness is restored, equity in access to all environmental goods and ecosystem services is assured through institutionalisation of people's participation"; and "a future in which the nation takes pride in the quality of its environment, forests, richness of its biodiversity, and efforts by the State and its people to protect, expand and enrich it, for intra and inter-generational equity and welfare of the local and global community".

(c) Recent Initiatives in addressing Pollution

The concern for environmental quality has heightened in the present scenario of rising population, increasing urbanisation, industrial pollution, shipping, aviation and vehicular emission as well as pollution of water resources due to discharge of industrial effluents and sewage without conforming to the environmental norms and standards apart from agriculture run-off. The Government had adopted the Policy for Abatement of Pollution in 1992, which provides multi-pronged strategies in the form of regulations, legislations, agreements, fiscal incentives and other measures, to prevent and abate pollution in various environmental media like air, water, soil, etc. The Government also adopted the National Conservation Strategy and Policy Statement on Environment and Development, 1992. These were followed by the National Environment Policy (NEP-2006) which seeks to extend the coverage, and fill in gaps that still existed, in light of extant knowledge and accumulated experience, laying emphasis on a number of new issues.

CPCB plays a vital role in abatement and control of pollution by generating environmental quality data, providing scientific information, rendering technical inputs for formulating national policies and programmes, training and development of manpower and organizing activities for promoting awareness at different levels of Government and public at large. It also provides support to various committees and authorities constituted by the Government, such as the Environmental Pollution (Prevention and Control) Authority for the National Capital Region. It co-ordinates activities under the Water (Prevention and Control of Pollution) Cess Act, 1977 and also enforcement and implementation of Rules framed under EPA, 1986 with SPCBs/ PCCs.

During the Twelfth Five Year Plan, the total outlay for CPCB is ₹ 380.00 crore. The Annual Action Plan (Work Plan) for 2013-14 laid emphasis on strengthening environmental monitoring network, carrying out random checks of industries for compliance verification, review of existing standards and development of new standards and inventory of wastes. Capacity development of SPCBs/ PCCs, through trainings and organizing/ participation in mass awareness programmes continued into 2013-14.

The key environmental concerns in India relate to air, water, land and soil, energy, biodiversity and ecosystem services. In India, National Ambient Air Quality Standards (NAAQS) were notified in the year 1982, duly revised in 1994 based on health criteria and land-use. These were revisited and revised in November 2009 for 12 pollutants, which include SO2, NO2, PM10, PM2.5, Ozone, Lead, CO,NH3, Benzene, arsenic, benzopyrene, and nickel. In 2012-13, ambient air quality monitoring stations were installed at 542 locations in 223 cities/ towns. Major developments in 2012-13 towards abatement of water pollution include water quality monitoring at 2,500 locations covering 445 rivers, 154 lakes, 12 tanks, 78 ponds, 41 sea water, 45 drains, 10 water treatment plants and 807 wells.

With regard to management of hazardous substances, the Ministry has notified E-Waste (Management and Handling) Rules, 2011, which have come into effect from 1st May 2012 and prepared the draft Notification on MSW (Management and Handling) Rules, which would be notified after completing the process of inter-Ministerial consultation. The Ministry has also notified the Bio-Medical Waste (Management and Handling) Rules in 1998, as amended (2000, 2003) to ensure that the bio-medical waste is handled without any adverse effect to human health and environment. The Rules contain provisions relating to segregation, packaging, storage, transportation, treatment and disposal of bio-medical waste. The Rules are applicable to all persons and institutions involved in generation and handling of biomedical waste in any form. As per these Rules, it shall be the duty of every occupier of an institution generating BMW, to take all steps to ensure that such waste is handled without any adverse effect to human health and environment. The Prescribed Authority for enforcement of provisions of these Rules is the SPCB/ PCC. The Prescribed Authority for enforcement of provisions in all health care establishments of Armed Forces under the Ministry of Defence is the Director General, Armed Forces Medical Services.

The Ministry has notified the Municipal Solid Wastes (Management and Handling) Rules, 2000 for effective management of MSW management. The Rules, inter alia, provide for criteria and procedure for MSW management by the municipal authority in the respective area of its municipality. The Rules apply to every municipal authority, which are responsible for collection, segregation, storage, transportation, processing and disposal of MSW. This Ministry has simultaneously initiated a project for 'Remediation of contaminated Hazardous Waste Dump Sites' under the National Clean Energy Fund. Twelve contaminated areas have been identified as priority sites in the country. This supplements the work being taken under the World Bank project.

A National Strategy on Hazardous Wastes Management has been formulated to facilitate effective management of hazardous wastes and implementation of the action plan brought out in NEP, 2006, so as to avoid environmental pollution and adverse health effects due to their improper handling and disposal. These strategies prescribe approaches and action points for regulatory bodies, generators of hazardous waste, recyclers and operators of facilities in order to minimise, recycle, treat and dispose of left over hazardous waste in an environmentally sound manner. This strategy will also facilitate fulfilling obligations under the Basel Convention and disposal of hazardous waste, including its minimisation, environmentally-sound management and active promotion of cleaner technologies.

(d) Initiatives in addressing Climate Change.

India is a Party to the United Nations Framework Convention on Climate Change (UNFCCC). The main objective of the Convention is to stabilise concentration of Green House Gas (GHG) of anthropogenic origin in the atmosphere at safer levels. Recognizing the country's vulnerability to human induced climate change, the Ministry has taken several actions to address climate change at the national level besides fulfilling its obligations under the UNFCCC.

The Government has conducted periodical assessments of climate change from scientific perspective with a view to determine domestic response to it. The Second National Communication (NATCOM) was prepared and submitted to the UNFCCC in May 2012. The NATCOM provides GHG emission inventory by sources and assessment of the projected vulnerability due to climate change on various sectors of the economy such as water, agriculture, forests and biodiversity, human health etc.

Many other activities are being initiated under the new thematic scheme titled 'Climate Change Action Programme (CCAP)' include the National Carbonaceous Aerosols Programme (NCAP), Long Term Ecological Observatories (LTEO), Coordinated Studies on Climate Change for North East Region (CSCCNER), National Institute for Climate Change Studies and Action (NICCSA), as a autonomous body of MoEF&CC, to support the Ministry/ Government in the area of scientific, technical and analytical studies relating to climate change and act as a nodal institution for Indian Network for Climate Change Assessment (INCCA). This institute will also conduct various scientific programmes on Climate Change; prepare NATCOM and Biennial Update Report (BUR), GHG inventory; develop projects on Nationally Appropriate Mitigation Actions (NAMA) and provide technical and analytical support to policy makers.

Besides, the Ministry has actively participated in review process and finalisation of Working Group Reports of fifth Assessment Report prepared by the Inter-governmental Panel on Climate Change (IPCC). The Summary for Policymakers of the IPCC Working Group-I AR5 titled "Climate Change 2013: The Physical Science Basis" was approved at the Twelfth Session of IPCC Working Group-I meeting held in Stockholm, Sweden, during 23-26 September 2013 and was released on 27

September 2013. Working Group-II on "Climate Change Impacts, Adaptation and Vulnerability" and Working Group-III on "Mitigation of Climate Change" are likely to be released in March 2014 and April 2014. The synthesis report comprising of key findings emerging from the three Working Groups of AR5, will be published by IPCC in October 2014.

Government of India is implementing the National Action Plan on Climate Change (NAPCC) which comprises of eight National Missions in specific areas of Solar Energy, Enhanced Energy Efficiency, Sustainable Habitat, Water, Sustaining the Himalayan Ecosystem, Green India, Sustainable Agriculture and Strategic knowledge for Climate Change. The Missions are under constant review of the Prime Minister's Council on Climate Change. Now, an Executive Committee on Climate Change under the Chairmanship of Principal Secretary to Prime Minister has been set up for assisting the Prime Minister's Council on Climate Change in evolving a coordinating response to issues relating to climate change, regular monitoring of the implementation of eight National missions and other initiatives on Climate Change and coordinating with various agencies on issues relating to climate change. Prime Minister's Office has entrusted the responsibility of convening and servicing the Prime Minister's Council on Climate Change as well as the Executive Committee to this Ministry. MoEF&CC is coordinating the implementation of envisaged activities under NAPCC and other initiatives by various Central Ministries.

(i) **National Solar Mission:** This mission aims at increasing the share of solar energy in the total energy mix through development of new solar technologies, while attempting to expand the scope of other renewable and non-fossil options such as nuclear energy, wind energy and biomass. The Mission targets include (i) deployment of 20,000 MW of grid connected solar power by 2022, (ii) 2,000 MW of off-grid solar applications including 20 million solar lights by 2022, (iii) 20 million sq. m. solar thermal collector area, (iv) to create favourable conditions for developing solar manufacturing capacity in the country; and (v) support R&D and capacity building activities to achieve grid parity by 2022. The Mission is to be implemented in three phases. It is envisaged that as a result of rapid scale up as well as technological developments, the price of solar power will attain parity with grid power at the end of the Mission, enabling accelerated and large-scale expansion thereafter. The Mission will have a focused Research and Development programme which seeks to address the India-specific challenges in promoting solar energy. Scheme wise financial outlay allocated for the 12th plan is ₹ 8795 crore.

For the first phase of the Mission, the Cabinet had approved a target to set up 1,100 MW grid connected solar plants including 100 MW capacity plants as rooftop and other small solar power plants till March 2013. In addition, a target of 200 MW capacity equivalent off-grid solar applications and 7 million square meter solar thermal collector area were also approved. The Cabinet had also approved setting up of large utility scale grid power plants through bundling of solar power with the unallocated thermal power available from NTPC stations and the policy to provide generation based incentive for small grid connected solar power plants.

The targets and achievements till 2013 under phase-I are given below:

Mission **Deliverables**	**Target for 2013-17**	**Target for 2013-14**	**Achievement in 2013-14**
Grid-connected solar power projects (Photovoltaic and Thermal)	9000 MW (3000 MW with Central support and 6000 MW under State initiative)	1100 MW Power Projects	522 MW
Off-grid solar power projects	800 MW	40 MW	22.7 MW
Solar heating – 70 lakh sq. meter of collector area	70	5	5

(ii) **National Mission on Enhanced Energy Efficiency:** This mission aims to achieve growth with ecological sustainability by devising cost-effective energy efficient strategies for end-use demand-side management. The mission aims to upscale efforts to create a market for energy efficiency. This Mission has 4 initiatives to create a conducive regulatory and policy regime to foster innovative and sustainable business models to unlock this market. These initiatives are (a) Perform, Achieve and Trade (PAT) (b) Market Transformation for Energy Efficiency (MTEE) (c) Energy Efficiency financing Platform (EEFP) (d) Framework for Energy Efficient Economic Development (FEEED). As a result of implementation of this Mission during five years, it is estimated that by 2015, about 23 million tons of oil-equivalent of fuel savings - in coal, gas, and petroleum products, will be achieved every year along with an expected avoided capacity addition of over 19,000 MW. The consequential carbon dioxide emission reduction is estimated to be around 98.55 million tons annually. The total fund requirement assessed for the 12th Plan Period for implementing the activities for the Mission is ? 190 crore.

The major deliverables of the Mission includes implementation of scheme/programme such as PAT, Bachat Lamp Yojana (BLY) program, Super-Efficient Equipment Programme (SEEP). These activities will lead to Greenhouse gas (GHG) mitigation in Industry sector, fuel switching and adoption of sector specific and cross cutting technological options. Mission has so far achieved the following:

- Commencement of the first commitment period of the PAT
- Global tender for super-efficient appliances has been called.
- Expansion of the energy efficiency financing platform through MoUs with public sector banks, implementation of Compact Fluorescent Lamp (CFL) programme.
- The operationalisation of the Partial Risk Guarantee Fund (PRGF) / Venture Capital Fund for Energy Efficiency (VCFEE) has been done.

(iii) **National Mission on Sustainable Habitat**: This mission attempts to promote energy efficiency in buildings, management of solid waste and modal shift to public transport including transport options based on biodiesel and hydrogen. This mission attempts to promote energy efficiency in buildings, management of solid waste and modal shift to public transport including transport options based on biodiesel and hydrogen. Prime Minister's Council on Climate Change had approved the mission document on June 18, 2010. The total fund requirement assessed for the 12th Plan Period for implementing the activities for the Mission is ₹ 950 crores, which is to be met from existing budget of Jawaharlal Nehru National Urban Renewable Mission (JNNURM). The National Mission on Sustainable Habitat (NMSH) seeks to promote:

- Improvements in energy efficiency in buildings through extension of the energy conservation building code - which addresses the design of new and large commercial buildings to optimise their energy demand;
- Better urban planning and modal shift to public transport - make long term transport plans to facilitate the growth of medium and small cities in such a way that ensures efficient and convenient public transport;
- Improved management of solid and liquid waste, e.g. recycling of material and urban waste management - with special focus on development of technology for producing power from waste;
- Improved ability of habitats to adapt to climate change by improving resilience of infrastructure, community based disaster management, and measures for improving advance warning systems for extreme weather events; and
- Conservation through appropriate changes in legal and regulatory framework.

The key deliverables of the Mission includes:

- Development of sustainable habitat standards that lead to robust development strategies while simultaneously addressing climate change related concerns;

- Preparation of city development plans that comprehensively address adaptation and mitigation concerns;
- Preparation of comprehensive mobility plans that enable cities to undertake long-term, energy efficient and cost effective transport planning; and
- Capacity building for undertaking activities relevant to the Mission.

Progress made so far against the given targets for the 12th Five Year Plan is given below:

(a) NMSH standards were developed for six sub-sectors namely
    (a) Solid Waste Management
    (b) Water and Sanitation
    (c) Storm Water Drainage
    (d) urban planning
    (e) energy efficiency and
    (f) urban transport for integration in developmental activities in the state. These standards have been circulated to state governments for inclusion in municipal bylaws and uploaded on Ministry's website.

(b) Energy Conservation Building code 2007 made mandatory for new as well as old buildings; incorporated in CPWD General Specification for Electrical Works in 2013.

(c) Green Building norms made mandatory for CPWD since 2009 and incorporated in CPWD Works Manual 2012.

(d) As per CPWD works Manual 2012, all CPWD construction shall henceforth be green and shall meet energy requirements for a minimum of 10 per cent of the internal lighting load.

(e) Specific guidelines have been issued for enhanced lighting system efficiency.

(f) Guidelines have been issued by CPWD for improving the resilience of infrastructure and improving the disaster warning system.

(g) More than 50 programmes are in various stages of implementation for capacity building.

(h) Advisories, Manuals and reports issued on recycling of solid and other waste including construction and demolition waste.

(i) Long term transport plan for cities has been prepared

(j) Metro Rail projects sanctioned (359.42 km) (outside Delhi)

(k) New Metro Rail projects under consideration having a length of 130.16 km

(l) Buses sanctioned under JNNURM for Mission Cities (15260 buses in 61 mission cities)

(m) Buses and ancillary infrastructure being sanctioned (9532 buses)

(n) Under the flagship programme of JNNURM/UIDSSMT following number of schemes sanctioned:

*760 nos. water supply projects at an estimated cost of ₹

5649.76 crore

*245 nos. sewerage projects at an estimated cost of

₹2063.42 crore

*108 nos. municipal solid waste management projects at

an estimated cost of ₹ 2367.03 Crore

*156 nos. storm water drainage projects at an estimated

cost of ₹ 10333.24 Crore

(iv) **National Water Mission**: This mission aims at conservation of water, minimizing wastage and ensuring equitable distribution both across and within states. Major components of this Mission are development of comprehensive water database and assessment of impact of climate change on water resources, promotion of water conservation, augmentation and preservation, focused attention to over-exploited areas, enhance water use efficiency by 20 per cent, and promotion of basin level integrated water resources management. The total fund requirement assessed for the 12th Plan Period for implementing the activities for the Mission is ₹ 89,101 crores. Proposals for ₹ 196 crores only have been approved. The status of implementation as of 31.12.2013 of the Mission is as below:

- The National Water Policy 2012 (NWP-2012) was adopted by the National Water Resources Council at its meeting held on 28.12.2012 under the chairmanship of Hon'ble Prime Minister. It provides for promotion of Basin Level Integrated Water Resources Management. The Ministry of Water Resources (MoWR) has constituted a Committee under the Chairmanship of Justice T.S. Doabia to examine the River Board Act, 1956 and suggest ways and means to meet the needs of the 21st century. Further, an integrated river basin approach, combining both surface and ground water, using advanced technology tools, would be adopted for water management and conservation.

- The MoWR has initiated action for preparation of State Specific Action Plans on Climate Change for Water sector. The Ministry has also formulated a National Project to undertake country-wide aquifer mapping to achieve community based management of aquifers covering about 8.89 lakh sq.km during the XII Plan. Emphasis will be on increasing public awareness and ensuring participation of stakeholders in water management.

- Central Water Commission (CWC) has completed a pilot study of basin-wise water situation in collabouration with the National Remote Sensing Centre (NRSC), Hyderabad for two basins, viz. Godavari and Brahmani-Baitarani. The studies are being extended to all the basins of country to be taken up by CWC and NRSC. Necessary support, guidance and training required for carrying out the above studies would be provided by NRSC. The detailed programme for carrying out the studies is under formulation in consultation with NRSC.

- CWC has launched Water Resources Information System (WRIS) with NRSC. The beta version of the system was posted on the web during December, 2010 (www.india-wris.nrsc.gov.in). India-WRIS Web GIS Version 2.0 was launched in March, 2012 containing water resources information of the country duly categorised and organised along with a toolkit for viewing purpose. Version 3.0 has been launched in December 2012. The updation of spatial and temporal coverage is a continuous ongoing process. The setting up of National Water Resources Information Centre (NWR-IC) is under process to manage the large volume of data on water resources and allied fields.

- A MoU has been signed between the Ministry of Water Resources and Asian Development Bank for a Technical Assistance with the objective to undertake operationally relevant research to identify and test integrated flood mitigation and flood plain management strategies for flood issues. The study identified Buri-Gandak River basin in Bihar and Baitarni River basin in Odisha to demonstrate strategies for coping with floods through community participation.

(v) **National Mission for Sustaining the Himalayan Ecosystem:** This mission aims at evolving management measures for sustaining and safeguarding the Himalayan glaciers and mountain ecosystem and is attempting to address key issues namely impacts of climate change on the Himalayan glaciers, biodiversity, wildlife conservation and livelihood of traditional knowledge societies. The total fund requirement assessed for the 12th Plan Period for implementing the activities for the Mission is ₹ 1,500 crores. Proposals for ₹ 500 crores have been approved. The deliverables and targets for the 12th Five Year Plan are given below:

Mission Deliverables	Target for 2013-17	Target for 2013-14	Achievement in 2013-14
Networking and Strengthening of knowledge institutions	12 institutions	4	4
Start of new centres relevant to Climate change in existing institutions in Himalayan states	10	3	4
Training in areas relevant to Himalayan ecosystem	100 persons	40	30
Training system for community based organisations to relate lab findings to real field	6 theme based	2	2
Training of technical experts in EIA	100	25	175
Capacity building programs/ training	25 programs	6	3
Development of Observational Network to monitor the health of Himalayan ecosystem	1	1	1
Regional Cooperation with neighbouring countries in Glaciology	All neighbours	1	1
Bi-annual advisories to Himalayan Sustainable Development Forum	At least 2 advisories	1	1
Annual thematic status report	6 theme based/year	6	6

(vi) **National Mission for a Green India:** This mission focuses on enhancing ecosystem services and carbon sinks through afforestation on degraded forest land in line with the national policy of expanding the forest and tree cover to

33 per cent of the total land area of the country. The total fund requirement assessed for the 12th Plan Period for implementing the activities for the Mission is Rs. 45,800 crores. Cabinet has approved ₹ 13,000 crores for implementation of various activities under the mission. The deliverables and targets for the 12th Five Year Plan are given below:

Mission Deliverables	**Target for 2013-17**	**Target for 2013-14**
Increase in quality of forest cover and ecosystem services (million hectare)	0.176	0.005
Restoration of ecologically challenged ecosystems (increase in forest cover) (million hectare)	0.0593	0.0016
Enhancing tree cover in Urban and Peri-urban areas (million hectare)	0.0066	0.0002
Agro forestry and social forestry (million hectare)	0.0987	0.0027
Wetlands (million hectare)	0.0033	0.0001
No. of Landscapes to be treated/area	130	4
No of landscapes to have enabling activities	1000	40
No. of households covered for enhanced livelihood on prorata basis (lakh)	0.15 Million household	

Mission Progress made so far:

* In the preparatory phase, 71 landscapes with a workable area of 1.77 lakh ha in 21 States have been identified. Preparatory activities have been undertaken which include setting up of mission organisation, awareness generation, micro-plan, baseline survey, preparation of perspective plan of the landscape, and entry point activities, etc.
* About ten States have already submitted their perspective plans at a total cost of ₹ 226 crores to be taken up in 33 landscape having working area of about 0.85 lakh ha.

* Most of the other States have identified landscapes and are at varying stages in preparation of perspective plan. The Plan proposals for preparatory phase in respect of Bihar, Mizoram, Meghalaya, Sikkim, and West Bengal States worth ₹ 33.60 crores have also been received.

States were sensitised regarding salient features of Green India Mission (GIM) and its approach through workshops. Regional workshops on operational guidelines were organised with the stakeholders including civil societies. Demonstration workshop on identification of landscape based on various parameters such as vulnerability map, forest cover, poverty etc. were held at FSI Dehradun inviting all the states. The progress on micro-plans and perspective plans for the identified landscapes, preparatory activities in additional landscapes, etc. has been reviewed.

(vii) **National Mission for Sustainable Agriculture:** The mission aims at enhancing food security and protection of resources such as land, water, biodiversity and genetics, through developing strategies to make Indian agriculture more resilient to climate change such as development of new crop varieties resistant to thermal, fire, drought etc., new credit and insurance mechanisms and improving productivity of rain-fed agriculture. The total fund requirement assessed for the 12th Plan Period for implementing the activities of the Mission is ₹ 1,08,000 crore. However, proposals for ₹ 13,034 crore have been approved so far. Taking into account the availability of funds, 15 deliverables are proposed for implementation under the Mission. The deliverables are Water Use Efficiency, Horticulture, Crop Sector, Seed, Pest, Disease and Weed Management, Soil Health Management, Farm Mechanisation, Conservation/ precision farming, Agriculture-Supply Chain Management, Safety Net, Credit, Access to Information, Research and Development, Capacity Building and Livestock and Fisheries.

(viii) National Mission on Strategic Knowledge for Climate Change: This mission is intended to identify the challenges of, and the responses to, climate change through research and technology development and ensure funding of high quality and focused research into various aspects of climate change. The total fund requirement assessed for the 12th Plan Period for implementing the activities for the Mission is ₹ 2,500 crores. However the expenditure to undertake these activities will be met out of the budget allocation of the existing scheme of the department. The deliverables and targets for the 12th Five Year Plan are given below:

Mission Deliverables	Target for 2013-17	Target for 2013-14	Achievement in 2013-14
Thematic Knowledge Networks	10	2	2
Technical Reports	12	2	11
Regional Climate Models	4 to 6	2	**3**
Chairs of Professorship	50 (25)	5	0
Specially- trained high quality CC Professionals	200	50	25
Public- Private Partnerships	3	3	0
Technology Watch Groups	11	5	2
Thematic Reports	5	2	3
International S & T partnership	5	2	2

State Action Plans on Climate Change and current progress

As a follow up to the Prime Minister's announcement in the State Environment Ministers' Meeting held in August 2009, the State Governments have been requested to prepare the State Action Plan on Climate Change (SAPCC) to provide linkage and to effectively implement the activities under NAPCC. SAPCC includes the current and future State's climate change scenarios and likely impacts of climate change of the concerned region on sectors such as water, agriculture, energy etc. Accordingly strategies are being identified and prioritised to address the issues of the vulnerable areas, sectors and communities and their associated risks.

So far, 26 States/UTs namely, Andaman and Nicobar Islands, Andhra Pradesh, Arunachal Pradesh, Assam, Chhattisgarh, Delhi, Haryana, Jammu and Kashmir, Jharkhand,

Kerala, Karnataka, Lakshadweep, Madhya Pradesh, Manipur, Meghalaya, Mizoram, Nagaland, Odhisa, Puducherry, Punjab, Rajasthan, Sikkim, Tripura, Uttarakhand, Himachal Pradesh and West Bengal have prepared their SAPCCs.

MoEF&CC follows a two stages process for giving final endorsement to SAPCC. In the first stage, draft report is considered by the Expert Committee on Climate Change (ECCC). On receipt of the revised SAPCC incorporating suggestion/ recommendation made by the Expert Committee on Climate Change, the National Steering Committee on Climate Change (NSCCC) considers and endorses the SAPCC. So far, nine SAPCC documents namely Arunachal Pradesh, Rajasthan, Madhya Pradesh, Sikkim, Tripura, Manipur, Mizoram, West Bengal and Andhra Pradesh have been endorsed by the NSCCC in May 2012 and April 2013. Further, 8 States/UTS namely, Haryana, Himachal Pradesh, Jammu and Kashmir, Kerala, Meghalaya, Nagaland, Odhisa and Puducherry have also been endorsed by the ECCC in its meetings held on October 10, 2013 and February 25, 2014.

'Climate Change Action Programme (CCAP)' a new thematic/umbrella Scheme of the MoEF&CC, has been approved by the Planning Commission for the XII Five Year Plan. The scheme aims at creating and strengthening the scientific and analytical capacity for assessment of climate change in the country. This scheme has a tentative outlay of ? 290 crore for 2012-17. The components of the scheme include supporting scientific assessments and studies relating to climate change, preparation and implementation of SAPCCs and NAPCC, creation of institutional structure for implementation and capacity building at the national and state level for implementing a low carbon strategy of development.

Government of India also participates in the negotiations on climate change under the auspices of the UNFCCC and its Kyoto Protocol. Besides, Government has also participated in other international fora on climate change, such as the BASIC

(Brazil, South Africa, India and China) group, Major Economies Forum, Petersburg Dialogue, and such other bilateral and plurilateral initiatives to protect India's long term interests. At the recent negotiations held from 11-23 November 2013 in Warsaw, a package of decisions were adopted with a view to advance the implementation of the UNFCCC and its Kyoto Protocol. India contributed constructively to these negotiations to ensure that future arrangements are built on equity and Common but Differentiated Responsibility (CBDR).

Carbon markets are an important mechanism established under the Kyoto Protocol to stabilise the GHG emissions across the globe as also to foster sustainable development in developing countries. India is a leading participant in the international carbon markets and, today, India projects represents a significant component of the global CDM market. As on 31 December 2013, India has the 2nd highest number of registered projects: 1,465 out of total 7,407 projects registered by the CDM Executive Board are from India.

(e) Addressing Bio-diversity related challenges.

Convention on Biological Diversity (CBD), a key agreement with near universal membership with 193 countries as its Parties, including India, was adopted during the Earth Summit held in Rio de Janeiro in 1992. It is the first comprehensive global agreement which addresses all aspects relating to biodiversity. It sets out commitments for maintaining the world's ecological underpinnings while pursuing economic development. It reaffirms sovereign rights of nations over their biological resources, and establishes three main goals: the conservation of biological diversity, the sustainable use of its components, and the fair and equitable sharing of the benefits arising out of the use of genetic resources.

India is a mega diverse country, with about eight per cent of the world's biodiversity, high percentage of endemic floral and faunal species, and four biodiversity hotspots. Taking cognizance of CBD, and to address the excessive pressure on biodiversity, the Government of India has enacted Biological Diversity Act, 2002 (BDA 2002). National, State and local level mechanisms have been provided for implementation of the Act. At the national level, National Biodiversity Authority (NBA) was established by Government of India on 1 October 2003 at Chennai (Tamil Nadu) under Section (8) of the Act. Following their establishment in Bihar, Maharashtra and Jammu and Kashmir, State Biodiversity Boards (SBBs) have now been established by all State Governments. Seventeen States viz. Andhra Pradesh, Arunachal Pradesh, Assam, Gujarat, Karnataka, Kerala, Madhya Pradesh, Maharashtra, Manipur, Meghalaya, Mizoram, Odisha, Rajasthan, Sikkim, Tripura, Uttar Pradesh, and West Bengal have notified the State-specific rules in accordance with the Section 63(1) of the Act.

The Biodiversity Act of 2002 provides for access and benefit sharing related to traditional knowledge and biodiversity. India has taken a number of proactive measures related to biodiversity conservation. Since 1991, the government has committed funds, particularly in the field of PA management, for eco-development (integrated conservation and development), along with site specific package comprising measures for conserving biodiversity through local community development. There have been some successful examples of the eco-development programme like the Periyar Tiger Reserve. In recognition of the need to protect the Western Ghats, a biodiversity hotspot, the MoEF&CC set up a Panel in 2010 to study its ecological status and recommend improvements which submitted its report in August 2011. Report of the high level working group on Western Ghats under the Chairmanship of Dr K Kasturirangan also submitted its report in April 2013, which is under the consideration of the Ministry.

(f) Monitorable socio-economic targets and goals in XIIth Plan.

Towards programmatic strategies for environment and forestry sectors, Ministry lays emphasis on improving forest cover, preserving wetlands, treatment of municipal solid waste and urban sewage, restoration of mining areas, community involvement in forest management, protection and preservation of biodiversity and wildlife and community rights and appropriate pricing of minor forest produce and addressing the challenges involved in mitigation and adaptation actions under climate change. The Twelfth Plan has identified 13 monitorable socio-economic targets for the Ministry and 14 goals which should receive special attention which are as below:

MONITORABLE SOCIO-ECONOMIC TARGETS

Environment and Climate Change

(1) Assess and remediate 12 identified contaminated sites (hazardous chemicals and wastes) with potential for ground water contamination by 2017.

(2) Clean 80 per cent of critically polluted stretches in rivers by 2017 and 100 per cent by 2020.

(3) States to meet National Ambient Air Quality Standards (NAAQS) in urban areas by 2017.

(4) To reduce emission intensity of GDP in line with the target of 20 to 25 per cent reduction over 2005 levels by 2020.

Forests and Livelihood

(5) Greening 5 million hectare (ha.) under Green India Mission including 1.5 million ha. of degraded lands, afforestation and eco-restoration of 0.9 million ha. of ecologically sensitive areas.

(6) Technology-based monitoring of forest cover, biodiversity and growing stock including change-monitoring on periodical basis through dedicated satellite by 2017 and establishment of open web-based National Forestry and Environmental Information system for research and public accessibility by 2015.

(7) Engagement of Village Green Guards/ Community Foresters for every Joint Forest Management (JFM) village by 2016.

(8) Establish forestry seed bank in forest circles and Model Nursery in every district with information on public portal by 2014.

Wildlife, Ecotourism and Animal Welfare

(9) Twenty per cent of veterinary professionals in the country will be trained in treating wildlife.

(10) Integrated Ecotourism District Plans covering 10 per cent of all potential Protected Areas (PAs) by 2017.

(11) Promoting participation of private sector, civil societies, NGOs and philanthropists in animal welfare.

Ecosystem and Biodiversity

(12) Restore 0.1 million ha. of wetlands/ inland lakes/ water bodies by 2017.

(13) Mapping and preparation of biodiversity management plans for deserts, coastal areas, important coral zones, wetlands, mangroves and so on to be completed by 2017.

GOALS

Environment

(1) Epidemiological studies to assess improvement in health status due to better management of environment and ecology.

(2) Promotion and adoption of cleaner technology, strengthening and initiation of reforms in regulations, policy making and enforcement institutions for environmental governance.

(3) Move towards cumulative and strategic EIA.

(4) Ensure ecological flows in all rivers by regulating abstractions so as to allow conservation of riverine ecosystems through developing a legal framework and management strategy for conservation of river basins.

(5) Promotion of recycling and reuse of treated sewage in urban projects such as sanitation, landscaping, central air conditioning and so on.

Forests and Livelihood

(6) Improve forest productivity, production and sustainable management of biodiversity (equity in access to benefit sharing with local people).

(7) Restoration and intensification of forest-rangelands/ grazing-land management and establish community grazing land around forest fringe villages.

(8) Build capacity of Village Forest Committees/ Joint Forestry Management Committees for management of forest resources including ecotourism.

(9) Revive seed orchards and silviculture plots for various forest types of the country as well as for enlisted species under Minor Forest Produce (MFP)/ Non-Timber Forest Produce (NTFP) including genetic improvement of and establishment of clonal orchards.

Wildlife, Ecotourism and Animal Welfare

(10) Reducing and managing human-wildlife conflict.

(11) Commercialisation of permissible marine products rich in poly unsaturated fatty acids (PUFAs), vitamins and so on.

(12) Promotion of ecotourism and participatory eco-development support livelihood of local population.

Ecosystem and Biodiversity

(13) Develop national targets and indicators related to biodiversity and support actions to strengthen implementation of Biological Diversity Act, 2002 and ensure bio-safety for economic and social development of local communities.

(14) Assess coastal biodiversity resources, ensure sustainable management, restoration of mangroves, coral reefs and wetlands and support livelihood.

(g) India's Stand in Rio+20 Summit (Prime Minister's remarks in the Summit).

The Rio+20 Summit on Sustainable Development is timely because it focuses our minds on "the future we want" and how to realise it. Difficult though it may seem, we have to summon the imagination to balance the costs that we will incur in the present with the benefits that will accrue to future generations. Economic Development, social inclusion and environmental sustainability are all equally critical as components of sustainable development. The task before us is to give practical shape and content to this architecture in a manner that allows each country to develop according to its own national priorities and circumstances.

For developing countries, inclusive growth and a rapid increase in per capita income levels are development imperatives. The 1992 Rio Summit correctly acknowledged that poverty eradication must remain the over-riding priority for developing countries. Those living at the subsistence level cannot bear the costs of adjustment and their livelihood considerations are important in determining how scarce natural resources such as land, water and forests are used. The severe deterioration of land and water resources is already affecting the well- being of millions of people living on the edges of subsistence, particularly women and children.

Sustainable development also mandates the efficient use of available natural resources. All the Countries have to be much more frugal in the way they use natural resources. A key area of focus is energy. We have to promote, universal access to energy, while, at the same time, promoting energy efficiency and a shift to cleaner energy sources by addressing various technological, financial and institutional constraints.

In India, we are implementing an ambitious National Solar Mission as a critical option for our energy security. Moreover, current consumption patterns in the industrialised world are unsustainable. We need to find new pathways for sustainable living. Environmental sustainability is the third leg of the sustainable development architecture. Economic activity invariably results in negative spinoffs, either by way of local pollution, or by way of global effects such as Greenhouse Gas emissions. We need to tackle both.

Local pollution can be regulated and such regulation may

impose costs on various economic actors. To ensure equity, there may be a case for targeted assistance to small producers to meet part of these costs and this should be built into policy. At the global level, our approach to the problem should be guided by equitable burden sharing. It is for this reason that the first Rio Summit enshrined the principle of common but differentiated responsibilities. India has reaffirmed this principle as well as the principle of equity during this Summit. This does not, however, mean that countries should not take proactive actions to promote sustainable development. In India, our efforts over the last two decades have yielded positive results. Over the period 1994-2007, our emissions-GDP intensity, excluding agriculture, has declined nearly 25 per cent. Looking ahead, we have set a target to further reduce the emissions intensity of GDP by 20-25 per cent between 2005 and 2020.

Many countries could do more if additional finance and technology were available. Unfortunately there is little evidence of support from the industrialised countries in these areas. One of the key challenges that demands urgent global action is the worrying depletion of biodiversity across our planet.

The Prime Minister concluded that future we want should be a future in which there is ecological and economic space for Sustainable growth for all and that we should attain the future that we all desire.

(h) Conclusion

Though India has made significant progress in terms of its achievements across the pillars of sustainable development, many problems continue to persist. New threats are also posing new challenges to the country. Though there has been reduction in poverty levels in the country, there is a need to step up efforts for further poverty eradication and inclusive development. The depletion of natural resources and deterioration in environmental quality needs to be addressed on an urgent basis.

India's air quality ranks among the lowest five countries in the world, according to a Yale University study that assessed 178 nations. The only countries ranked below India on this score are Pakistan, China, Nepal and Bangladesh. The report assessed countries on their air quality, status of biodiversity, water and sanitation. Overall, India's rank was 155th, far below other BRICS countries, China (118), Brazil (77), Russia (73), and South Africa (72). In the report, India ranks 127 in terms of human health from environmental damage and in air quality where it ranks 174, barely above Pakistan, China, Nepal and Bangladesh. "India's air quality is among the worst in the world, tying China in terms of the proportion of the population exposed to average air pollution levels exceeding World Health Organisation thresholds" said a statement by Yale University.

The topic of environmental problems and solutions is quite complicated and difficult to understand given the complexity/interrelations of different components of the ecosystem. It is however, the attitude/approach of human beings towards using the natural resources that is going to influence environment to a great extent. The knowledge of environmental ethics should also help in the conservation of natural resources.

CHAPTER-4

ECO TAXES IN OTHER COUNTRIES

INTRODUCTION

The world faces enormous environmental challenges. Our environment has been threatened by industrialisation and improved standard of living. Problems of pollution and ecological degradation are not confined to national states but they also impact on living conditions on entire globe. The urgency of reducing greenhouse gases to curb climate change has been documented by the Intergovernmental Panel on Climate Change and is underlined by the Stern Review: The Economics of Climate Change, which sums up the situation with the statement that "The scientific evidence is now overwhelming: climate change is a serious global threat, and it demands an urgent global response". The conclusions of the Stern Review give strong messages on the economic impacts:

- Climate change could have very serious impacts on growth and development.
- The costs of stabilising the climate are significant but manageable; delay would be dangerous and much more costly.
- Actions on climate change are required across all countries, and it need not cap the aspirations for growth of rich or poor countries.

We have to acknowledge the fact that our environment is an essential and irreplaceable resource for our survival. Environment has been under attack since the beginning of industrial age. We have been unable to effectively eliminate the erosion and decay of our environment. National and international communities are showing increased engagement to find solutions for environmental problems such as global warming, water and air pollution. Albeit, environmental problems are common, such problems have not received commensurate attention by legislators/policy makers. Legislators/policy makers have many tools at their disposal to encourage or discourage individual or corporate behaviour/attitude towards environment. One available tool is tax policy, which is often designed to discourage or encourage citizen and corporate action to protect and improve environment. The solutions must be tailored to the fiscal, cultural and political realities in each nation.

Environmental taxes, often called eco taxes or green taxes, enhance environmental protection and provide a source of additional governmental revenues. When eco taxes are imposed, the individual has option to either reduce damage to environment or pay the eco taxes commensurate to the environment. Since the cost of compliance is lower and more advantageous to the individual vis-à-vis payment of eco taxes, the individual voluntarily complies and resulting in positive change in behaviour towards environment.

Eco taxes are particularly effective because they function to internalise externalities, provide incentives for consumers to change behaviour, raise revenue, and pass those costs on to consumers of the end product or service through higher prices. Without internalisation, the full economic costs of activities are not factored into the prices of goods and services, thereby causing large market distortions. With eco taxes, however, all external costs, direct and indirect, are paid for by the polluter (and ultimately, the consumers of the polluter's product or service), leading to an efficient reallocation of the burden of pollution. In other words, environmental taxes lead to "fair and efficient" prices by re-distributing costs.

During recent years, eco taxes have become increasingly popular in many countries in Europe. In these countries, eco taxes are supported by a number of different stakeholders because they conform to the "polluter pays" principle. This is a fundamental fairness rationale that makes environmental taxes popular in some quarters. Eco taxes provide incentives for polluters to change their behaviour, and for consumers to use less of the taxed product. Although some environmental taxes target consumers, others target producers, ultimately, all of the costs associated with any given tax are passed on to the consumers of the environmentally harmful products or services. Environmental taxes minimise pollution control costs because they don't require costly government oversight. All of the management decisions are in the hands of the polluter-it must decide whether it is cheaper to pollute and pay the associated taxes, or to devise a more environmentally-friendly way of doing business. Under such a regime, those polluters that face higher costs for pollution reduction techniques will be more likely to pay the tax, while those who can reduce pollution more cheaply will be more likely to choose that option. Therefore, results will still be achieved without costly monitoring or oversight by the government. Eco taxes encourage innovation because producers have an incentive to find alternative, more environmentally-friendly means of production.

In 1991, at Earth Summit in Rio de Janeiro Conference, it was felt that one of the challenges facing the world is that of global climate change caused by global warming. One of reasons of the causes of global warming identified was the atmospheric pollution. The main sources of atmospheric pollution are: (a) combustion of fuels to produce energy for heating and power generation in the household and industrial sectors; (b) exhaust emissions from the transport vehicles that use petrol, diesel oil, etc., and (c) waste gases, dust and heat from many industrial sites including chemical manufacturers and electrical power generating stations. The Rio Convention on Climate Change included an agreement to reduce significantly the emission of greenhouse gases by all parties to the Convention. The method adopted by the European Union (EU) was taxes on energy, and direct taxes on CO2 emissions. According to the OECD 2006 Report, a database operated in cooperation between OECD and the European Environment Agency (EEA) has entered 375 environment related taxes in OECD member countries, plus some 250 environmentally related fees and charges in those countries. Of these taxes, the largest number is levied on energy products (150), on motor vehicles (125), and various forms of waste (50).There is a wide range of environmentally related taxes currently levied in the OECD-countries, among others: water pollution tax, batteries tax, logging tax, tyres tax, beverage container tax, toxic waste levy, tax on plastic bags, aircraft noise tax, tax on groundwater extraction, tax on pesticides and artificial fertilisers, landfill tax, ozone depletion tax, etc.

Eco tax reform in different countries across the globe mainly aims at shifting the tax burden from factors of production, such as labour and capital to pollution and use of natural resources (EC, 1997). Eco tax reforms have been mainly carried out in countries of Europe, New Zealand, Canada, etc. The predominant emphasis in eco tax has been on energy and transport. Over the years new tax bases have been added. For instance, waste end taxes in Norway and New Zealand, and annual car taxes differentiated according to environmental characteristics in Germany.

Eco-Tax in selected countries:

a. Norway

Norway has a long experience with environmental taxation since 1931, when petrol tax was introduced. It was followed by tax on sulphur in mineral oil in 1971. Taxes have been introduced to reduce environmentally harmful emissions to air and water, and to reduce the amount of waste generated. However, a wide-spread use of environmental taxes was not witnessed until the late 1980s and early 1990s. Taxes on mineral fertilisers, pesticides and lubricant oil were introduced in 1988, CO2 tax on petrol, auto diesel oil, mineral oil and the petroleum sector (only offshore) in 1991, while the sulphur tax on mineral oil was increased substantially. Since the early 1990s tax instruments have played an important role in providing incentives for cleaner production and consumption patterns, even though regulation has remained the main policy instrument to abate environmental damage.

In Norway, 4.2 per cent of central government tax revenue is due to environmental and energy taxes, equivalent to 1.6 per cent of GDP (estimates based on the 2006 budget). A main part of this revenue is taxes on energy consumption, not only having an environmental purpose, but nevertheless having a positive impact on the environment. The level of green taxation is one of the highest in the OECD area. Environmental taxes, as discussed in the following, refer to taxes with an explicit environmental purpose (e.g. CO 2 and sulphur taxes).

Box 1. Environmental taxes in Norway - main developments

1971	Sulphur tax on mineral oil
1974-1993	Tax on non-refillable beverage containers (replaced by broader taxation of beverage packaging)
1986	Petrol tax differentiated according to lead content
1988-1998	Tax on nitrogen and phosphor in mineral fertilisers
1998	Tax on pesticides, tax on lubricating oil
1990-1991	Tax on environment damaging batteries (replaced by regulation)
1991	CO 2 tax on petrol, auto diesel oil, mineral oil (excl. fisheries etc.), and petroleum sector (only offshore activities)

1992-2002	CO 2 tax on coal and coke, except most industrial processes
1994	Environment tax on beverage packaging differentiated according to return rate
1999-2001	Sulphur tax on coal, coke and oil refineries at a low rate (replaced by voluntary agreement)
1999	Tax on final waste treatment. CO 2 tax includes domestic sea transport of goods (formerly only passenger transport) and the supply fleet
2000	Tax on environment and health damaging chemical products (only two products so far), beverage packaging tax differentiated according to materials, auto diesel oil tax differentiated according to sulphur content, annual weight-based tax on heavy vehicles differentiated according to emission standards (Euro I-Euro III)
2003	Taxes on HFCs and PFCs

Source: Ministry of Finance, Norway.

In January 2007, a new environment tax on nitrogen oxides (NOx) was imposed in Norway. The introduction of the tax was deemed necessary in order for Norway to meet the obligations under the Gothenburg Protocol and reduce NOx-emissions by 2010. The main sources of such emissions in Norway are the domestic shipping, petroleum extraction, road transport, the coastal fisheries and certain industries. Although the tax rate at the introduction was at the low level of 15 NOK per kilo, and for practical reasons only energy production by larger engines and plant in sectors representing 55 per cent of the emissions were targeted, it was deemed necessary to couple the tax with significant compensatory payments to support certain affected industries whilst also establishing subsidy arrangement in support of other direct measures to reduce NOx-emissions.

b. United Kingdom

I. **Climate Change Levy (CCL):** A tax on energy use by

business and industry was announced in the 1999 Budget and implemented in April 2002. It was announced earlier to give businesses time to adjust their practices. It is a tax on business use of energy. Its aim is to provide incentives for energy efficiency, reduced consumption and switching to low emission fuels that do not attract a tax. The CCL is charged at different rates according to the type of fuel supplied and its energy content. Rates of levy are equivalent to 0.15 pence per kWh for natural gas and coal, 0.43 pence per kWh for electricity, and 0.07 pence per kWh for liquefied petroleum gas (LPG).

The revenues from the CCL peaked at £832 million in 2003-04 after which it declined subsequently showing an overall improvement in energy use. Revenue has started increasing again after 2007 probably due to the increase in the tax rates. Around three quarters of total revenue comes from the supply of electricity and a quarter from the supply of natural gas. Solid and other fuels generate very small revenues each year. Revenues from CCL have been recycled to the business sector by a reduction in employer's National Insurance contributions by 3 percentage points. This has shifted tax burden to energy and away from labour costs. A study undertaken by Cambridge Econometrics estimated that CCL reduces overall energy demand in the economy by 0.2 per cent in 2000, 1 per cent in 2001, 1.8 per cent in 2002 and 2.9 per cent by 2010 compared with a situation where the CCL package had not been announced or implemented.

II. **Landfill Tax:** This tax was introduced in 1996 with objective to reduce the negative externalities emanating from waste disposal. Waste disposal adversely affect health due to methane emission, contamination of water systems, etc. Commercial entities involved in waste disposal are required to pay at a standard rate of £7 per ton on waste delivered to landfill sites. A lower rate of £5 per ton applies to inactive wastes. The standard rate was increased to £10 in 1999. Further, annual increase in rate @ £ 1 per ton from 2000, resulted into final level of £15 per ton in 2004. The total tax collections in 2001-02 were £502 million. In 2008-09 revenue realised from landfill tax amounted to £954 million.

III. **London Congestion Charge:** The congestion charge was introduced in Central London by Greater London Authority in 2003 in order to reduce the level of congestion. The charging zone is an area of 22 sqkms. The charge is applicable to any vehicle (with exceptions of taxis, buses, emergency services vehicles, vehicles used by registered disabled, vehicles using gas, electric, fuel cells) entering or parking in the zone between 7 am and 6.30 pm on a weekday. The charge was originally set at £5 per day, but was increased to £8 in 2005. It is estimated that around 150,000 drivers are eligible to make the payment each day. The net revenue from the congestion charge was £137 million in the year 2007-08. By law, this revenue has to be invested back into the London's transport system.

The monitoring report of Traffic for London (2006) suggests that congestion has fallen by around 25-30 per cent relative to pre charging baselines. This charge has also reduced carbon emissions by around 16 per cent within the charging zone by allowing traffic to flow more freely and reducing time spent idling in traffic queues and it is likely to increase demand for public transport by around 1-2 per cent.

IV. **The aggregates levy:** Aggregates refer to rock, gravel, sand and any materials naturally mixed with them and normally payable by the quarry operators and other organisations that commercially exploit aggregates. It was introduced in 2002 at £1.60 per ton. Imported aggregates are also charged when they are commercially exploited. This tax is charged to take account of the external costs of aggregates extraction. These externalities include emissions from transportation, noise, dust, pollution of groundwater, loss of habitat for wildlife, etc. A part of the revenue from the levy goes to this fund to be used to minimise the demand for aggregates, promote environmentally friendly aggregates extraction and reduce the local effects of extraction. The revenue for 2008-09 is £334 million or 0.07 per cent of the total tax revenues for that year. The total amount of aggregates extracted fell from 266.5 million tons in 2003-04 to 224.4 million tons in 2008-09, a fall of around 15 per cent. The sales of aggregates fell by 8 per cent between 2001 and 2003 in spite of increasing construction activity. During the same period estimated production of recycled aggregates in England increased by 3.1 million tones.

V. **Vehicle Excise Duty (VED):** The VED is an annual tax on road vehicles first introduced in 1889. Till 1999, a flat rate tax was charged. In June 1999, this flat rate was reformed into a two tier system where, small cars with an engine size of less than 1,100cc paid a lower tax of £100 per year, while larger cars paid £155. In 2001, system of graduated VED (GVED) was introduced. Four bands based on the emission rating of the vehicle were introduced (Bands A to D). An additional band E was later added in 2002 and band F in 2003. In 2006, a seventh band G was added and the tax charged on cars with the lowest emission rating (Band A i.e. 100g or les of CO2 per km) was reduced to 0. Tax required to be paid under Band G was £210. Further reforms took place in the Budget of 2008. The number of bands for 2009 was increased to 13, Bands A to M. From 2010 onwards, a new system was introduced where news cars will be charged a different VED for the first year in which they are bought. This rate will be higher than standard rate for cars with high emissions and lower for cars with low emissions. Revenue from VED has increased steadily since the reforms of 2001. The revenue for the year 2008-09 is £5600 million which is 1.28 per cent of the total tax revenues of that year.

VED represents a fixed cost of car ownership. As such, it does not give an incentive to drive less. Instead, it provides an incentive to buy more fuel efficient cars and encourages motorists to scrap older and more polluting cars. Study has shown that the average emissions rating of new cars purchased have been declining over the years. It has reduced from 190 g/km in 1997 to 165 g/km in 2007, a drop of 13 per cent (Butcher, 2009). This is still far above the EU target of 140 g/km by 2008-09. Further evidence has shown that since 1997, there has been a changing of consumer preferences away from cars that come under higher bands.

VI. Fuel Duty: While VED is a fixed cost of ownership of vehicle, 'fuel duty' is an eco-tax on the actual use/travel undertaken by the vehicle. As the need for travelling is often inelastic, eco-tax is observed to have made no major impact on the air pollution level. In terms of revenue generation, fuel duty is the largest source of green tax revenue. The fuel duty yielded £24,615 million in 2008-09, which is 5.64 per cent of the total tax receipts.

In the long run, it also encourages people to buy more fuel efficient cars. The impact of fuel duty on driving depends on the own price elasticity of demand for petrol which is in turn affected by the availability and price of substitutes such as public transport and alternative fuels. Studies suggest that a 10 per cent rise in the price of fuel reduces fuel consumption by around 2.5 per cent and traffic volume by 1 per cent after a year, all other things remaining constant (Leicester, 2006).

VII. **Air Passenger Duty (APD):** The APD was introduced in 1994. It is a tax levied on airlines based on the number of passengers flying domestically or internationally from UK airports (other than flights from the Scottish highlands or the Islands). The APD is a relatively small tax in revenue terms. Its effectiveness depends on the price elasticity of air travel which has been estimated by studies to be quite low. A Canadian review estimated that a 10 per cent increase in price would reduce demand for long haul business flights by 2.5 per cent and short haul business flights by 7 per cent.

VIII. **Motor fuel Differentiation:** It was introduced in 1987 in favour of unleaded petrol at 0.96 pence per liter. In 1997, it was upwardly revised to 4.8 pence per liter by 1995. It was primarily introduced to offset the higher cost of unleaded petrol and later to provide an incentive for fuel switching. Leaded petrol was removed from market in 2000.

IX. **Water Abstraction Charge:** It is levied by the Environment Agency to cover cost incurred in water resource management. It is paid by businesses that extract and use over ground water, underground or tidal water sources.

If a tax system is environmentally effective in inducing desired outcome of reduced consumption of the 'bad', it leads to erosion of tax base itself - resulting in fall of tax revenue. Decline in revenues could also occur because the system of eco-taxes is in its infancy. Taxes on inelastic goods are levied for revenue purposes; increased revenue need not mean high environmental effectiveness.

C. Germany

I. Energy Tax: The objective of introduction of energy taxes in Germany is to reflect the true economic cost of energy use (i.e., internalise the externalities) and use the revenue to promote employment by reducing the cost of labour. Germany undertook eco tax reform between 1999 and 2003. The eco tax reform between 1999 to 2003 in Germany comprises of (a) raising energy tax and (b) introduction of tax on electricity. Accordingly, mineral oil taxes on transport fuels were gradually increased by €154 per 1,000 liters for gasoline and diesel, amounting to a thirty-one per cent increase on gasoline and forty-eight per cent increase on diesel. The taxes on light heating fuels were increased by fifty per cent and the tax on natural gas was doubled during the same time period. Taxes on heavy fuel oil increased in 2000 and again in 2003.Through this reform, Germany expected to raise its revenue.

The eco tax revenue was primarily used to reduce non-wage labour costs put towards public pension scheme or to limit their increase. In 2003, the revenue generated by the eco-tax amounted to approximately 18.7 billion Euros, from which 16.1 billion, i.e. about 90 per cent, went into the public pension scheme. Employers and employees could thus benefit from a reduced contribution rate, from 20.3 per cent in 1998 to 19.5 per cent in 2005.

II. **Packaging Ordinance:** In January 2003 Germany introduced a compulsory deposit on non-recyclable drinks packaging between 0.1 to 3 liters in volume containing mineral water, beer, soft drinks and alcoholic mixed drinks. The compulsory charge is 25 cents. The deposit has stabilised the proportion of recyclable drinks packaging and put an end to the throw-away mentality. Fruit and vegetable juices, milk and wine, as well as ecologically favourable non-recyclable drinks packaging - such as cartons, polyethylene bags and stand-up bags - are deposit-free.

III. **Vehicle Tax:** In July 2009, Germany introduced reformed car taxation with objective of reducing CO2 emission from road traffic. The new system combines the previous taxation based on cylinder capacity (at a lower rate) and a CO_2 component, which charges a tax of Euro 2 per gram of CO_2 emissions per kilometer (g/km) if those exceed a threshold of 120 g/km. Under the new tax scheme, cars with higher cylinder capacity or fuel consumption are taxed higher than under the previous tax scheme: A petrol powered car in the mini segment with low fuel consumption (i.e., CO_2 emissions of less than 120 g/km) is subject to an annual tax of approximately Euro 20 only, while a luxury car with a relatively high cylinder capacity and fuel consumption is subject to charges between approximately Euro 300 and Euro 400. The revenue from car taxes currently amounts to almost EUR 8 billion (the total taxes on road vehicles amount to approximately Euro 8.8 billion), at an average tax of Euro 200 per car.

d. Sweden

I. **Carbon Tax:** Carbon tax was introduced in Sweden in 1991 which is levied on oil, coal, natural gas, and liquefied petroleum gas, petrol and aviation fuel in domestic traffic.

The carbon rate was 27 Swedish kroner (SKR) per metric ton of CO2 in 1991 which was later increased to 108 SKR per ton in 2009 (Branlund and Kristrm ,1997). The most obvious impact of introduction of the carbon tax has been the increased use of biomass. The use of biomass has been increased in industry since 1990 from 45 Terrawatt-hour per year (TWh/yr) to 54 TWh/yr. The most important result of the taxation system is the development of methods of biomass extraction and a biomass market and increase in the biomass demand. The energy tax on fossil fuels, are high and it acts as a powerful complement to the carbon tax.

II. **Vehicle Excise Duty:** Vehicle Excise Duty was introduced in Sweden in 2006. Annual excise duties have been based on the economic performance of vehicles. The duty is comprised of a base charge of 360 SKR plus a CO2 charge of 15 SKR per gram of CO2 exceeding 100 grams per kilometer (g/km). The carbon dioxide emissions have been reduced in 2003 when compared to 1995. The increase in the number of green cars is the result of environmental vehicle duties and the establishment of the concept of green cars has been quite successful. The use of eco friendly car has been increased from 52 per cent in 2003 to 66 per cent in 2006. From July 2005 to 2006, the total share of more efficient cars increased from 2.9-12.8 per cent.

e. Belgium

Energy Tax: The Belgian government had organised a roundtable in early 1993, which concluded that the energy tax was the favoured instrument to achieve the desired economic improvement given its revenue potential and the ensuing employment gains. Belgium introduced energy tax on gasoline, heating oil and electricity in 1993. These new taxes, which raised the price of a liter of gasoline but were not applied to industry. Consequently, consumers bore the full burden. The revenue received from these taxes allowed reduction in employers' social security contributions paid by manufacturing firms, whose export competitiveness had suffered.

f. New Zealand

I. **Waste Levy:** It is estimated that every year, New Zealanders generate around 3.2 million tons of waste material to landfill. It was felt that there is need to improve environmental performance by taking responsibility for the waste by finding more effective and efficient ways to reduce, reuse, recycle or reprocess it. In order to move forward, in 2008, the Waste Minimisation Act 2008 was introduced to encourage waste minimisation and decrease waste disposal in New Zealand. This Act imposes $10 per ton (excluding GST) levy on all waste sent to landfill and it is effective from 1st July 2009. The objective of introduction of this levy is to create funding opportunities for waste minimisation initiatives and provide an economic incentive to polluters to change their behaviour.

The levy encourages people and organisations to rethink how they dispose of waste and reward efforts made to divert material from landfill. Placing this cost on waste helps us to recognise the true social, economic, and environmental impacts and costs that waste has on people and the environment. The levy will be charged at facilities where waste (including household waste) is disposed of and which operate, at least in part, as businesses which dispose of waste. Half of the levy money will go to territorial authorities (city and district councils), on a population basis, to spend on promoting or achieving the waste minimisation activities set out in their waste management and minimisation plans. A waste minimisation fund will be set up with the remaining levy money, minus administration costs, to fund waste minimisation projects. Projects will be assessed according to a set of criteria established in consultation with the Waste Advisory Board. The Minister for the Environment has final approval on project funding.

II. **Road User Charges:** The charge is set at a rate which recovers the cost that heavy vehicles impose on the public road system. The money collected is used for maintenance and construction of the road system, traffic enforcement and safety programmes.

III. **Fuel Excise Duty:** Excise duty is a charge imposed by the government on certain products sourced from overseas and some products produced within New Zealand. The following motor spirits are entitled for refund of the excise duty and the goods and services tax (GST) charged: (a) fuel in an exempted vehicle, (b) fuel in a road user charges-licensed vehicle, (c) fuel in a commercial vessel, and (d) for commercial purposes other than as fuel in any motor vehicle, vessel, or aircraft. Agricultural vehicles, some mobile machinery and commercial vehicles that don't travel on the road are exempt vehicles. The types of fuel eligible for a refund are motor spirits, CNG and LPG. The following fuel types are not eligible for a refund (i) any fuel used for a motor vehicle that's used principally in vehicle races, trials, or other sporting events, (ii) fuel used in recreational boats and pleasure craft, (iii) fuel that has already had excise duty refunded, and (iv) diesel. The funds will be used for improving road and public transport.

IV. **Motor Vehicle License Fee:** All the revenue collected from fees goes to the public road system, to pay for road construction and maintenance, traffic enforcement, and road safety programmes.

V. Voluntary Initiatives

(a) **Recycling:** The New Zealand Packaging Accord is a voluntary initiative to cut down on wasteful packaging. Those signing it - the packaging and packaged goods industry, local and central government and the recycling operators - are voluntarily committing to doing what they can to reduce the proportion of packaging in our total waste stream. On 7th September 2009, The Packaging Council released the latest data about New Zealand's packaging production, consumption and recovery showing that New Zealanders recycled more than 428,000 tones of packaging last year. Since 2004 the total quantity of packaging recycled increased by 26 per cent, whereas consumption of packaging increased at a much slower pace by 14 per cent. On a per capita basis the quantity recycled by every New Zealander increased by from 83 kg to 100 kg.

(b) **Product Stewardship:** Product stewardship can increase resource efficiency. It requires producers to bear financial cost for the end-of-life waste management costs of their products and encourage them to take actions that reduce these costs, such as eliminating excessive packaging or components that are costly to recycle. It could extend to improved design so that fewer resources are used by a product in its everyday function. Further, Product stewardship schemes often have a focus on take-back mechanisms for the products. The development of these mechanisms can result in economies of scale for recycling operations, leading to increased resource recovery. Good design can also help the 'de-construction' of products and the recovery of materials. It shifts the burden for managing wastes on to those who produce the products and those who buy them. In this way it helps to internalise the environmental costs involved in managing products through their life cycle. Internalizing these costs provides economic incentives to use resources efficiently. It is also in keeping with the polluter-pays principle. The efficiency with which a product uses resources is also an important feature of design. Better design for this can provide improvements in other areas. For example, reducing the number of components and having fewer different materials in the product can improve product reliability as well as making resource recovery from the used product easier.

g. Canada

In Canada, both the federal and the provincial governments share the responsibility of environmental policy. As such, environmental policy and tax rates differ among the provinces. Canada has not had much experience with environmental taxes. Fuel tax seems to be the most important eco tax. Fuel in Canada is subject to the Goods and Services tax/Harmonized Sales Tax (GST/HST), the federal excise tax, provincial taxes and provincial sales taxes. In addition to this, British Columbia also levies a carbon tax.

(I) Federal Tax on Fuel

The federal government charges three types of taxes on fuel. One is the royalty tax; a tax on companies that dig oil out of the ground. The federal royalty increases from 1 to 5 per cent of gross revenue over the first six years of production or until the initial investment has been recovered. After that, the royalty is either 30 per cent of the net cash flow or 5 per cent of gross revenue, whichever is greater. The second tax charged by the federal government is the GST/HST. For the year 2009, the GST is 5 per cent and the HST 13 per cent. Besides, royalty and the GST/HST, the federal government also charges an excise tax on fuel.

(II) Provincial Taxes on Fuel

Each province has a separate tax for fuel. Thus, the price of fuel is different in each province. An important provincial tax is the recently introduced carbon tax in British Columbia.

(a) British Columbia's Carbon Tax

This tax is levied on the purchase and use of fossil fuels such as gasoline, diesel, natural gas, heating fuel, propane, coal, etc. The tax is payable by all individuals and businesses who buy fuel in British Columbia and by producers and manufactures of fuel who use their own fuel in the production process. The carbon tax rate is different for each fuel. It depends on the fuel's emission of CO_2 equivalent (CO_2e). CO_2e is the amount of carbon dioxide, methane and nitrous oxide released into the atmosphere, with the non carbon dioxide emission levels adjusted to a carbon dioxide equivalent basis. Since the carbon tax is designed to be revenue neutral, this revenue will be returned to the public through reductions in other taxes.

(b) Quebec, Canada

Quebec introduced carbon levy in October 2007. The carbon levy is \$3.20 (C\$3.50) per ton of CO_2. The level is readjusted every year based on the volume of sales. The rate varies for each fuel, with the gasoline levy at \$0.0076 (C\$0.008) per liter, diesel fuel at \$0.0086 (C\$0.009) per liter, propane at \$0.0048 (C\$0.005) per liter, and coal at \$7.64 (C\$8.00) per ton.

Revenues generated from carbon levy will be earmarked for a "green fund", which supports, among others, reductions of GHG emissions in public transport, financially supporting the capture and combustion or valorisation of landfill gas, supporting manure processing and biomass and supporting research and innovation for carbon sequestration.

III. Vehicle Tax

(a) Federal Excise Tax

There is a federal excise tax on fuel inefficient automobiles. This is based on the weighted average fuel consumption rating, which is calculated by combining 55 per cent of the city fuel consumption rating with 45 per cent of the highway fuel consumption rating. The rates for automobiles with a rating of 13 or more liters per 100 kms are given below:

- o at least 13 but less than 14 liters per 100 km - \$1,000
- o at least 14 but less than 15 liters per 100 km - \$2,000
- o at least 15 but less than 16 liters per 100 km - \$3,000
- o 16 or more liters per 100 km - \$4,000

(b) Tax for Fuel Conservation, Ontario (TFFC)

The TFFC was introduced in 1989, after which it has been reformed many times. It is a flat tax on fuel inefficient vehicles in Ontario. It is levied on passenger vehicles using 6 liters or more gasoline or diesel per 100 km and on sports utility vehicles using 8 liters or more. The TFC rates vary according to the fuel use rating of a car.

IV. Deposit-refund Scheme in Yukon

Since 1992, Yukon Territory in Canada has been implementing a deposit -- refund Scheme. Consumers, when they buy beverage containers, are required to pay a deposit. Consumers get a refund when they return the empty container to one of about 25 registered recycling depots in the territory. Beverage wholesalers send the deposit to the Recycling Fund, which then reimburses recycling centers for refunds made, collection, processing and shipping costs. During the period 2000-2001 the return rate for containers was found to be nearly 85 per cent.

V. Tire Stewardship Programs in Canada

Tire Stewardship is a not-for-profit programme to manage the scrap tire recycling under the different provincial waste reduction Acts and regulations. Industry stewardship organisations established under these regulations operate externally from government. The aim of product stewardship is to find better methods of diverting or reducing the amount of designated materials as landfill wastes by encouraging industry producers to consider improving end-of-life management for the materials they design, manufacture and sell. This is achieved by bringing greater levels of responsibility to the producers and users of the materials and products. Broadly, they strive to achieve the following objectives:

- Operate a program that ensure timely, cost efficient collection of all scrap tires from all parts of the province without user fees at the point of collection.
- Ensure adequate processing capacity to prevent build-up of backlogs of whole or partially processed scrap tires.
- Promote economically viable end uses and market

applications for scrap tires.

The details of Tire Stewardship programme in different provinces are as follows:

Province	Year of launch	How it works
Alberta	1992	Consumers pay a $4 fee for every passenger car and truck tire they buy, which funds the collection, transportation and recycling of tires. Collection Method: Registered tire processors pick up waste tires. Consumers can also drop off scrap tires at designated collection sites.Who runs it: Alberta Recycling Management Authority
British Columbia	2007	Consumers pay a fee ranging from $5 to $35 for each tire purchased, which funds the scrap tire recycling program (including transportation and recycling of tires). Collection Method: Consumers can drop off scrap tires at participating tire retailers (retailers aren't required to collect scrap tires, though). Who runs it: Tire Stewardship BC.
Manitoba	2008	Consumers pay an Eco fee ranging from $4.50 to $75 for each tire purchased, which funds the scrap tire recycling program. Collection Method: Consumers can drop off

		scrap tires at designated tire processors or arrange for them to be picked up. Who Runs It: Tire Stewardship Manitoba
New Brunswick	1996	Consumers pay a fee ranging from \$3 to \$13.50 for each tire purchased, which funds the scrap tire recycling program. Collection Method: Consumers can drop off scrap tires at any tire retailer in NB. Commercial operations with a large number of tires can arrange for them to be picked up. Who Runs It: Recycle NB
Newfoundland/ Labrador	2002	Consumers pay a fee of \$3 t o \$9 for each tire purchased, which funds the scrap tire recycling program. Collection Method: Consumers can drop off scrap tires at any tire retailer or other designated outlets. Who Runs It: Multi Materials Stewardship Board
Nova Scotia	1997	Consumers pay a fee of \$3 to \$9 for each tire purchased, which funds the scrap tire recycling program.Collection Method: Consumers can drop off scrap tires at any tire retailer in NS. Who Runs It: Resource Recovery Fund Board
Ontario	2009	Consumers pay a fee

		ranging from $5.84 to $250.20 for each tire purchased, which funds the scrap tire recycling program. Collection Method: Consumers can drop off scrap tires at registered collectors, which include retailers, municipalities and other drop-off points. Who Runs It: Ontario Tire Stewardship
Prince Edward Island	1999	Consumers pay a $4 fee for each tire purchased, which f unds the scrap tire recycling program.Collection Method: Consumers can drop off scrap tires at registered retailers.Who Runs It: Island Waste Management Corp.
Quebec	1993	Consumers pay a $3 fee for each tire purchased, which funds the scrap tire recycling program. Collection Method: Consumers can drop off scrap tires at tire retailers. Who Runs It: Recyc-Québec
Saskatchewan	1996	Consumers pay a fee ranging from $4 to $75 for each tire purchased, which funds the scrap tire recycling program. Collection Method: Retailers collect old tires when they put new ones on consumers' vehicles; there's currently no free disposal/ collection option. Who Runs

		It: Saskatchewan Scrap Tire Corp.
Yukon	2007	Consumers pay a fee ranging from $5 to $35 for each tire purchased, which funds the scrap tire recycling program (including transportation and recycling of tires). Collection Method: Consumers can drop off scrap tires at participating tire retailers. Who Runs It: Tire Stewardship Manitoba

Source: Environment Compliance Insider, Canada.

h. Denmark

Denmark initially targeted households, by increasing taxes on waste and recycling the revenue through reductions in income tax. Subsequently, in 1996, industry was targeted with energy taxes introduced alongside reductions in social security contributions. Since 1999, the tax burden has been shifted further by raising environmental and corporate taxes but reducing personal taxes.

i. Finland

Finland introduced a carbon dioxide tax in addition to other energy taxes specifically targeting carbon emissions. However, electricity generation was exempted and gas was subjected to a 50 per cent reduction. Benefits were skewed towards households despite industry being equally affected by the new taxes. Revenues raised from green taxes have been used to partially offset revenue losses stemming from cuts made in taxes on labour.

j. The Netherland

The Dutch system of energy taxation consists of four taxes. These taxes are : (i) the general fuel charge (ii) the regulatory tax on energy (iii) the excise tax and (iv) the strategic oil storage tax. The general fuel charge was introduced in 1988 as part of an integral system for financing environmental policy expenditures. Its revenues were used for environmental expenditures. In 1992, however, the charge was transformed into a tax and became part of general tax revenues. As such, it fell under the administration of the Ministry of Finance. The general fuel tax is collected on all fossil fuels. Fuels used as raw materials are not subject to the tax. Under the general fuel tax, electricity is not taxed, though fuels used to produce electricity are taxable. Energy-intensive industries used to benefit from preferential rates under this tax but later this benefit was withdrawn.

The regulatory tax on energy came into force on January 1, 1996. In contrast to the general fuel tax, the regulatory tax on energy was introduced to alter behaviours towards greater energy efficiency, the revenue objective being of only secondary importance. The regulatory tax on energy focuses on small users of energy. A tax free allowance exists, which is set at 800 m^3 of natural gas or 800 kWh of electricity per year. The tax rate follows the European Community's first proposal of a CO2/energy tax of USD 10 per barrel of oil equivalent, Tax rates for the various fuels are then based on their CO2/ energy content. Fuels used to power road vehicles are not subject to the tax as they are covered by excise duties. Special exemptions are meant to induce energy efficiency; thus heat supplied via district heating and electricity produced with natural gas or renewable are exempt from the tax. In addition, natural gas used in greenhouses is exempt from the regulatory tax on natural gas to preserve the international competitiveness of the flower- and vegetable- growing sectors. The Netherlands has recycled increased energy tax revenue into both lower income tax and employers' contributions alongside reduction in corporate tax, greater tax credits for small business and increases in tax free allowances.

k. USA

Environmental policy in the United States is implemented predominantly through the command-and-control regime. The policy pursued by the authorities to meet environmental challenges posed by air, water, and solid waste pollution is mainly command-and-control in nature-federal prohibitions, regulatory rules and guidelines, standards, technical assistance, monitoring, and enforcement. Some states, however, enact their own environmental legislation to deal with unique and pressing environmental issues.

The command-and-control regime to combat environmental problems began in 1970 with the enactment of Federal National Environmental Policy Act, the Clean Air Act, and the establishment of Environmental Protection Agency. Regulations, standards, or procedures are enforced at the federal or state agency level. There is also growing realisation that direct regulation is costly and inefficient. Therefore, use of economic instruments in form of environmental taxes, subsidies, and tradable permits, are also being used as popular alternative. Due to higher cost of enforcement and inherent limitation in causing positive change in public behaviour/attitude, economic instruments has found greater acceptance among environmentalists, corporations, and the general public. The market-based instruments are being used in conjunction with regulation.

Among the few green taxes imposed in the United States at the federal level are the "gas guzzler" tax on new cars that exceed fuel efficiency standards, a tax on ozone-depleting substances, and miscellaneous taxes on fertilisers and pesticides used in agriculture.

I. The Ozone-Depleting Chemicals Tax- the federal excise tax on ozone-depleting chemicals was enacted to address the problem of emissions of ozone-depleting chemicals that harm the stratospheric ozone layer and leave the earth more susceptible to harmful ultraviolet radiation. Under the international Montreal Protocol, countries including USA agreed to phase out the use of key ozone depleting chemicals.

The U.S. federal excise tax supplements U.S. obligations under the Protocol. The tax neatly correlates the tax base which consists of 20 known chemicals having ozone-depleting characteristics and the tax rate to the environmental problem. The tax rate varies according to the ozone-depleting potential of each chemical. For example, CFC-11 has an ozone-depleting factor of 1.0 whereas Halon- 1301 has a factor of 10.0, causing the tax on the more potent Halon-1301 to be ten times greater. Thus, the tax base and the tax rate link directly with the chemicals' potential to damage the environment. From an administrative feasibility perspective, the tax was logically imposed on the manufacturers, producers, and importers of the chemicals at the time of their sale or use.

II. The Gas Guzzler Tax-following the oil embargo, the tax was enacted in 1978 to reduce reliance on imported oil. Its existence today is directly relevant to the environmental problems caused by carbon dioxide and other emissions from motor vehicles' combustion of gasoline, including climate change. The tax applies to automobiles based on their fuel economy, which is a significant factor contributing to the level of emissions, and the tax rate appropriately increases as fuel economy decreases. The tax rate starts at $1,000 for vehicles with fuel economy less than 22.5 but more than 21.5 miles per gallon, and it rises with each one-mile decrease in fuel economy until it reaches $7,700 for vehicles with fuel economy less than 12.5 miles per gallon. In terms of administrative feasibility, the tax is imposed on the manufacturer at the time of sale, but to preserve the environmental awareness and behavioural impact of the tax, dealers must place a notice about the tax on the sticker price for the car.

The environmental effectiveness of the tax, however, has been eroded significantly by the fact that it does not apply to "non-passenger vehicles," a term that now encompasses sport utility vehicles (SUVs). Part of the original 1978 law, this exemption was created long before SUVs were contemplated as a common choice for everyday travel, but the failure to amend the law to adjust to new circumstances has significantly undercut its force as an environmental instrument. In addition, the tax rates have not been increased since 1990, nor have the fuel economy thresholds been changed since 1978. If an environmental tax is intended to serve a long-term environmental purpose, the tax rate should be indexed for inflation or adjusted periodically to preserve its incentive effect and policymakers should consider adjustments to the definitions and thresholds that determine the tax base.

III. In the United States, environmental taxes are also imposed at the state level. For example, Arkansas imposes taxes on tires and batteries. Texas imposes coastal protection fees on crude oil. New Jersey has introduced fees for discharges into waterways. California levies a waste-water discharge permit fee.

Some observations can be made following a review of the recent experiences of European countries who are eco tax leaders.

First, the eco tax leaders did not carry out reform of green taxes in a vacuum. Rather, they have adopted these reforms against the common background of the Kyoto Protocol and other international agreements to cut greenhouse gas emissions in response to growing evidence of global warming. The lead role played by some countries, such as Norway, in the international arena assured a prominent position for eco tax reform on the domestic policy agenda. And because the OECD and European Union have taken innovative steps toward eco tax reform, these organisations have become key focal points for discussions and information exchange on these issues among developed countries. Indeed, the EU has adopted a separate burden-sharing agreement to enable its member countries to meet the targets under the Kyoto Protocol.

Second, the introduction of taxes on carbon dioxide emissions has been the common key element of all the eco tax reforms. All the countries have found that the most efficient way to reach environmental goals is through taxes targeting emissions of carbon dioxide-by far the dominant greenhouse gas. But because it is difficult to accurately measure carbon dioxide emissions, taxes are imposed on the estimated carbon content of the products emitting this gas. So, in practice, these taxes fall somewhere in between product taxes and pure emissions taxes. Tax rates vary markedly across the eco tax leaders, with Norway and Sweden having by far the highest rates.

Third, the main objective of eco tax reforms is not generally generation of large amounts of revenue. In most cases, these reforms have double aim of improving environmental conditions and using the funds raised to ease distortions created by other taxes-especially taxes that adversely affect employment. For example, the introduction of eco taxes allowed Denmark to cut marginal tax rates on labour income and social security contributions. And Sweden implemented a major general reduction in income taxation.

Fourth, studies show that the public perceives green taxes to be regressive. But at their current levels, eco taxes generally do not seem to have any major regressive impact. Also, the distributional consequences of green taxes should be measured in relation to the taxes they replace (often, labour taxes-which can be heavily regressive) and in terms of the environmental improvements they generate.

Fifth, a typical eco tax may well involve trade-offs that are lacking in other types of taxes: there is frequently a conflict between the fiscal and environmental goals of eco taxes since most eco taxes aim to eliminate or reduce their own tax bases. For example, high excise taxes on leaded gasoline caused this fuel to disappear from the market in Austria, Denmark, Finland, Norway, and Sweden. But as this example shows, eco taxes may change consumption patterns (in this case, gasoline consumption) by giving the consumer incentives to substitute cleaner for highly polluting products, while keeping intact a fairly stable and large tax base (in this case, unleaded gasoline).

Sixth, the conflict between fiscal and environmental goals becomes an issue only at certain levels of taxation and should, therefore, not be exaggerated. For instance, the tax base for many taxes on carbon dioxide emissions seems to be stable or even growing in countries using these taxes. And, the current levels of these taxes are not likely to change consumer habits in any major way. There also seems to be broad scope for adding new or raising existing taxes on pollutants. This could, of course, change in future with increased use of these taxes.

Seventh, initially Scandinavian countries were leaders in adopting environmentally related taxes. Later on other countries have also pursued the same approach, amongst them Germany and Italy. Further, environmental tax is gaining ground in Europe. United Kingdom has announced "climate change levy" and France has also introduced energy taxes. Finally, the scope of several existing reforms is scheduled to broaden, in particular by raising the green taxes paid by firms to bring rates closer to those paid by households. It can be mentioned that poorly-designed environmental tax reform can impose substantial costs on the economy. On the other hand, a well-designed reform can increase employment and distributional effects. The weight of economic evidence suggests that, for most economies, elements of good design include a labour tax reduction, ideally targeted at lower-wage workers to maximise employment benefits and offset distributional problems; policies to protect the competitiveness of energy-intensive industries; measures to prevent a wage-price inflationary spiral; policies to promote the development and diffusion of new cost-effective clean technologies; and policies to compensate low-income households outside of the workforce.

CHAPTER -5

ECO TAXES IN INDIA

Protection and preservation of environment is rooted in our culture heritage. Yajnavalkya Smriti, a historic Indian text on statecraft and jurisprudence written before the 5th century AD, prohibited the cutting of trees and prescribed punishment for such acts. Kautalya's Arthashastra, written in Mauryan period, emphasised the need for forest administration. Ashoka went further, and his seventh Pillar Edicts expressed his view about the welfare of environment and biodiversity. It expresses that "Happiness in this world and the next is difficult to obtain without much love for the dhamma, much self-examination, much respect, much fear of evil, and much enthusiasm. Beloved-of-the-Gods, King Piyadasi (Ashoka), speaks thus: Animals were declared to be protected - parrots, mainas, aruna, geese, wild ducks, nandimukhas, gelatas, bats, queen ants, terrapins, boneless fish, vedareyaka, gangapuputaka, sankiya fish, tortoises, porcupines, squirrels, deer, bulls, okapinda, wild asses, wild pigeons, domestic pigeons and all four-footed creatures that are neither useful nor edible. Also protected were nanny goats and sows which are with young or giving milk to their young, and so are young ones less than six months old. Cocks are not to be caponised, husks hiding living beings are not to be burnt, and forests are not to be burnt either without reason or to kill creatures. One animal is not to be fed to another. Our king killed very few animals."

Since Independence, India has lost 5.3 million hectare of forest to deforestation and huge amount of its mangroves forest. Most of it being chopped down for housing, industrialisation and river projects. It is estimated that the number of mangrove forests have more than halved in the last 20 years. Seventy per cent of the surface water in India is polluted due to uncontrolled dumping of chemical and industrial waste, fertilisers and pesticides. The extensive use of scarce natural resources and increasing pollution levels has led to huge greenhouse gases emissions (GHG). In January 2014, the Yale Environmental Performance Index ranked India 174th out of 178 countries on air pollution. According to India's Central Pollution Control Board, in 2010, particulate matter in the air of 180 Indian cities was six times higher than World Health Organisation standards. The World Bank says that environmental degradation is costing India $80 billion annually and accounts for 23 per cent of the nation's child mortality. The bank estimated that reducing particulate emissions by 30 per cent by 2030 would save India $105 billion in health-related costs. Environmental challenges are persistently increasing the pressure on governments to look ways to mitigate environmental damage while minimising harm to economic activities.

Protection of environment is the responsibility of both the government and the citizens in India. The government of India has taken a number of regulatory measures over the years to conserve the forests and to keep the environment pollution free. our Environmental policy in India, like the United States is traditionally rooted in command-and-control regime. The policy pursued by the authorities to meet environmental challenges posed by air, water, and solid waste pollution is mainly command-and-control in nature. The environmental laws enacted in India such as The Wildlife (Protection) Act 1972, Forests (Conservation) Act 1980, The

Water (Prevention and Control of Pollution) Act 1974 and The Air (Prevention and Control of Pollution) Act 1981 as well as the various Rules emanating from them are in the nature of 'command-and-control` regulation. While there may not be much scope for market based instruments (MBI) in the case of wild life protection, there is certainly good scope for employing market instruments for controlling water effluents, air pollution and waste disposal.

Although, most of these regulations are, in the nature of 'command and control` (CAC), Governments also have a range of environmental policy tools at their disposal, which are market-based instruments (such as taxes and tradable permits), negotiated agreements, subsidies, environmental management systems and information campaigns. Although no single instrument can be considered best to address every environmental challenge, there has been a growing movement towards environmentally related taxation (and tradable permits) in various economies. After the 1992 Rio conference, employing market-based instruments (MBIs) to promote environmental objectives have become increasingly popular. The term MBI covers a wide range of instruments including eco taxes. As we have just discussed in previous chapter, advanced economies of the West have been moving increasingly towards market-based approaches to environmental control. These new approaches allow individuals or companies greater flexibility in deciding where, when, how or to what extent to cut pollution emissions, thereby reducing the cost to the economy and increasing personal freedom. If properly designed, national market-based systems allow reductions of total national pollution emissions with greater flexibility and with lower cost than with less flexible and comprehensive approaches.

International experience has demonstrated that eco taxes can be very effective in their environmental impact. In a study by Sterner (2007) has concluded that "had Europe not followed a policy of high fuel taxation then fuel demand would have been twice as large". Further, if has also become clear that eco taxes did have a strong incentive value.

A good example is the case of leaded and unleaded petrol in European countries. When fiscal benefits for unleaded petrol were introduced, leaded petrol disappeared. Taxation and tax differentiation proved to be very efficient tools for the promotion of fiscal and other Community policies, as they have such a strong incentive value. Eco taxes should be complemented by eco subsidies. Eco subsidies may be given to producers and consumers for favouring goods and services that have environmentally benign impact. Internationally, there are several examples of eco subsidies. In Netherlands, rebate is given for replacement of old electrical appliances. In Italy, consumers receive a tax rebate for purchase of energy efficient refrigerators and freezers. In many EU countries, purchase of compact fluroscent lamps (CFL) is encouraged through subsidies.

The study of environmental regulation in developed countries, clearly shows that they are increasingly resorting to MBI like eco taxes to protect environment. They are doing so in conjunction with Command- and-control (CAC) approach or in preference to CAC approach. India may also take lessons from experiences of these countries for environmental regulation. India is also facing severe environmental pressure in pursuance of its development agenda. Increasing population growth and urbanisation has radically impacted the ecology.

It has been well known since 1920 when A.C. Pigou first published The Economics of Welfare that externalities cause economic inefficiency. Charging the full social cost of pollution gives firms and individuals the incentive to pollute less when the cost of pollution abatement is less than the social cost of pollution. One way of internalizing external costs is through eco taxes. Such taxes cause polluters or resource users to pay for the environmental resources they use, just as they pay for capital and labour. Environmental taxation has a significant role to play in addressing environmental challenges. Taxes can be extremely effective when they are properly designed, are levied as close to the environmentally damaging pollutant or activity as possible, and are set at an adequate rate.

The revenues generated can be used to help with fiscal consolidation or reduce other tax rates. Environmental taxes give rise to distributional or competitiveness concerns, but these are usually best addressed through other policies tools. Providing information, transparency, and certainty is critical to public acceptance and to the effectiveness of environmental taxation.

Finally, taxes may need to be combined with other instruments to obtain the most efficient and effective environmental policy package, but care should be taken to assess the impact of overlapping instruments.

Tax differentiation involves a positive charge being levied on a polluting product and a negative charge, or subsidy, on a cleaner alternative. The most common example of this tax differential is in the context of transport to discourage purchases of polluting vehicles or fuels. Less tax on compressed natural gas (CNG) vis-à-vis petrol in Delhi is one such example. By making dirty fuels like oil and coal more expensive, a carbon tax encourages utilities, businesses and individuals to reduce energy consumption and increase energy efficiency. A carbon tax also makes clean, renewable energy from sources such as wind and solar more cost-competitive with fossil fuels.

In 2007, the Madras School of Economics (MSE) under the guidance of Prof. Raja Chelliah had suggested for introduction of grade wise 'cess on coal' differentiated by the ash content in coal. The following grade wise rates on cess on coal were recommended by MSE:

	Grade/Type of Coal	Rate (₹ per tonne)
(A)	Coking Coal	
(i)	All verities if coking coal where ash content is 18 per cent or less	nil
(ii)	All varieties of cooking coal where ash is content is between 19 to 28 per cent	₹ 20
(iii)	All varieties of cooking coal where ash content is more then 28 per cent	₹ 40
(B)	**Non-Coking Coal**	
(i)	All verities of non-cooking coal where ash content is less then 28 per cent	nil
(ii)	All varieties of cooking where ash content is higher than 28 percent	₹ 50

The Union Budget (2010-11), announced the establishment of National Clean Energy Fund (NCEF) for promoting clean energy technology in the country. The NCEF was envisaged to be funded through imposing a cess on coal at the effective rate of Rs.50 per tonne for both domestic coal and imported coal. The clean energy cess is presently levied on coal, peat and lignite for the purpose of financing and promoting clean energy initiatives and funding research in area of clean energy. However, this was not in line with MSE's proposal recommending imposition of grade wise cess on coal. According to the study of MSE, reduction in ash content could be brought about through selective mining and beneficiation of coal. Currently, the cess on coal is imposed on the gross quantity of raw coal dispatched from a coal mine and no deduction is allowed on account of washing/ beneficiation of coal and details of which may be seen at Annex.

The accumulated reserves in the NCEF has crossed ₹ 1000 crore. The notification on Clean Energy Cess dated 22.06.2010 as well as the office memorandum of Tax Research

Unit (TRU), Department of Revenue do not, however, specify the manner the funds from NCEF have to be utilised. The revenues generated for NCEF may, be preferably utilised for setting up infrastructure units for coal washing, for selective mining, and for identifying activities for gainful utilisation of coal ash. The Union Budget (2014-15) has proposed to increase Clean Energy cess from ₹ 50 to ₹ 100.

Eco taxes have many advantages, such as environmental effectiveness, economic efficiency, the ability to raise public revenue, and transparency. Also, eco taxes have been successfully used to address a wide range of issues including waste disposal, water pollution and air emissions. Regardless of the policy area, the design of eco taxes and political economy considerations in their implementation are crucial determinants of their overall success. Following areas may be brought under the ambit of eco-taxes in India on similar lines as other countries:

Eco-Tax on Water Effluents

Industries in the area of chemical, fertilizer, paper, textile, cement, steel, petroleum, mining, coal and power sectors in India are required to pay a 'cess on water' for water consumed under The Water (Prevention and Control of Pollution) Cess Act, 1977. The rate of cess varies from ₹ 0.015 to ₹ 0.019 per litre of water (i.e. ₹ 15 to ₹ 19 for 1000 litres of water) depending on the nature of industry. The total revenue raised from the water cess amounted to ₹ 250 crore in 2012-13. The water cess so imposed is, however, in the nature of user charges (and is not an eco tax). The proceeds of this cess go to the Consolidated Fund of India. Subsequently, it is disbursed by the Government of India to State Pollution Control Boards based on the amount of water cess collected in the respective states. A portion of the fund is earmarked for the expenditure of the Central Pollution Control Board.

Organisations like New Delhi Municipal Corporation (NDMC) in New Delhi have been charging for the waste water/effluents released in their drainages at half the rate charged for the supply of fresh water. The charges so made for effluents released in NDMC drainages are not high enough to discourage entities consuming water to either (a) reduce their water consumption or (b) set up plants to clean them and recycle them. However, effluents released by various industries as well as by different agglomerates continue to be a major environmental concern in various cities and towns.

With regard to urban agglomerates and small scale industries (SSIs), however, there is no such compulsion. The responsibility of treating waste water in such cases has been fixed upon municipalities/state governments. The Government of India, in this context, has been supplementing the efforts of state governments through Central Plan schemes and Centrally Sponsored schemes.

Since the cost of treating waste water currently works out to ₹ 6-7 per Kilolitre (KL) of waste water, the eco tax on disposal of waste water may be fixed close to ₹ 10 per KL (notwithstanding the social cost in terms of adverse impact on health and hygiene). At such a rate of eco tax, it would be advantageous for these urban households to set up on their own plants rather than pay the eco-tax (on untreated effluents) to the government/local body/NDMC.

In the case of highly populated urban agglomerates with hardly any space for parks and gardens, such treated (waste) water could be given back to the supplying agency that may purchase this water and pay for it depending upon the purity of water. In case of unwillingness to set up such waste water treatment plants, such urban agglomerates/households will pay the eco tax equal to the (metered) amount of effluents. This would provide a ready source of funds to the local bodies/ the government for implementing environment friendly measures. Norms for rainy seasons may be suitably modified as the dynamics of water availability and the need for cleaning (waste) water undergoes a big change.

It is worth recognising that on a price of ₹ 15 per litre for bottled drinking water, the revenue earned from sale of 1000 litre/1KL works out to ₹ 15, 000. Against this, the current user charge for 1KL of clean water ranges between ₹ 15 to ₹ 19 and half this rate (as charged by NDMC) for disposal of waste water. In other words, water supplied by public utilities is highly underpriced and imposition of eco-tax may not be an issue. At the same time, gain to society from control and mitigation of pollution in terms of health and hygiene will be immense.

Eco-tax on Congestion

Congestions on road are observed to be the cause of higher air pollution. Many cities in the world impose a congestion charge on certain part of the city area, where density of vehicular traffic is very high. To discourage traffic in such areas, congestion charge is applied to vehicles entering in specified area. For example, in the central area of London, an entering vehicle (except ambulances) is charged a congestion tax of £8. This is applicable from 7 am to 6 pm, every day except Sunday. With a view to reduce traffic in peak hours (and in preferred market places), various countries have imposed 'congestion tax' on vehicle traffic. This may be introduced in India as well especially in metropolitan cities. One of the attendant benefits of this tax is that of raising resources to finance construction of flyover and bye-lanes to ease traffic movements.

Eco-tax on emission from Plants and Industries

Under the Environment Protection Act (1986), the Government of India has notified the emission standards for different industries. These notifications are, however, in the nature of 'command and control'. The policy instrument of eco-tax on emission from various industries has yet to be attempted in India. This would require installing of metres to measure the emissions. The normative standards- permissible limits of pollution - can be made more stringent under an eco tax regime to reward the better performers. A differentiated eco tax based on the recommendations of the expert group may, furthermore, be introduced to induce people to adopt various options to reduce the severity of pollution.

Eco-Tax on Old Vehicles

Old vehicles are observed to be the cause of 40 per cent of vehicular pollution in India. Eco-tax has been successfully utilised in France (and other countries) to gradually remove 'old vehicles' from roads. This may be done in India. In most cases a compounded system of motor vehicle tax exists where a onetime levy is paid for the life of vehicle. This does not make any distinction between pollution impacts of old vehicles. The motor vehicles tax should be levied every five years and older vehicles should be subjected to higher eco-cess every five years. After 15 years vehicles should be compulsorily taken out of road.

Government of Maharashtra in India has taken some initiative in this direction by imposing a green tax on old vehicles. Receipts from this green tax to the Government of Maharashtra amounted approximately to ₹ 125 crore per annum. While public and private vehicles (petroleum) more than 8 to 15 years old have to pay between ₹ 200-400 per annum year, vehicles more than 15 years old have to pay between ₹ 400 to 600 per year. Green taxes on diesel run vehicles are higher than these rates. It is felt these rates could easily be raised to ₹ 2000 and above per year. These green/ eco-taxes may be, furthermore, supplemented with the schemes of tax rebates (by both the Union Government and the State Governments) on purchase of new vehicles if the buyer offered his/her old vehicle in lieu of the new vehicle purchased. The governments could retrieve their respective losses of revenue through sale of scrap.

Property Tax Concession

The construction of 'Green buildings' may be encouraged by property tax concession. A rating mechanism called 'Griha' (Green Rating and Integrated Habitat Assessment' has been developed by the The Energy and Resources Institute (TERI) and Ministry of New and Renewable Energy on inputs from Ministry of Power's Energy Conservation Building Code.

Waste Management and Eco Tax

Both industry and households generate wastes, and consequently cause water, soil and air pollution. Wastes have become a huge problem in larger cities as they lead to contamination of water systems, bad odour, methane emission and health hazard. Imposition of waste levies is observed to induce people to economise on waste and also recycle them as far as possible. While such a waste levy brings about a behavioural change in both enterprises and households vis-a-vis disposal of wastes, it provides the much needed financial resources to the municipalities/authorities for better waste management.

In New Zealand significant positive impact of environmental taxes particularly levy has been to avoid waste, along with funding to help develop waste minimisation infrastructure, such as reprocessing facilities and collection system. Many commercial enterprises in OECD countries requiring disposal of wastes have to register with the concerned administrative/municipal/revenue department. All enterprises liable to pay a landfill tax in U.K pay such a tax (@ ₹ 500 per tonne for inactive wastes and @ ₹ 7,200/- per tonne for active wastes. Landfill tax need not be, however, paid for (a) dredging activity, (b) quarrying and mining, (c) pet cemeteries and (d) inactive waste for filling quarries. India may also think of levying waste management and may start with big cities.

Eco tax on Plastics

It is estimated that roughly 3000 tonnes of plastic waste is stated to be generated everyday in India. Although, plastics serve the useful purpose of carrying bags, packaging material and water bottles, they are an environmental hazard given their non- biodegradable nature. A promising usage of this non-biodegradable material has been found in being mixed with bitumen for road construction as well as in being mixed with cement. Their proper collection may, however, require incentivising rag pickers for segregating the plastic waste from general wastes. An eco-tax @ ₹ 1/- per water bottle has, furthermore, often been recommended that can be claimed as tax credit on depositing the empty bottles. This would be in the nature of deposit-refund system and may be introduced in India.

Eco-tax on IT Wastes

Given the high pace of innovation in the IT sector and their short life cycles, the IT sector has been witness to a high level of waste. Unlike plastics, consumer durables in the IT sector are quite often health hazards as it uses mercury, silica and lead. Under such circumstances, all the more, the government may use the policy instrument of 'eco-tax'. An eco-tax equal to `x' per cent of sale price may be imposed on these products that may be reclaimed by the buyers on depositing their machines as wastes. This would also be in the nature of deposit-refund system and may be integrated with the Extended Producer Responsibility. The government may, furthermore, notify the manner of their disposal under the waste management system.

Eco-tax on Aggregates (Sand, Gravel and Rock)

Unbridled mining of sand, gravel and rock from river beds, sea bed or ground can be very damaging to environment. An "aggregate levy" is therefore, being imposed on quarry operators (and similarly placed commercial enterprises) in U.K. since 2002. On import of such "aggregates" also, the aggregate levy is imposed.

India may also impose such a levy on all aggregates. The broad objective of such a levy is to (a) discourage extraction of aggregates, (b) promote environment friendly extraction and (c) reduce the local effects of such an activity. The experience of U.K in this regard shows that imposition of eco-tax on aggregates gave encouragement to recycling of products.

Some local/State Government Initiatives

The Uttarakhand Government has recently taken a decision to impose eco tax upon entry of tourist vehicle into the hill station of Mussoorie. It will be in line with the Naini lake tax charged from tourists in Nainital. The tax of ₹ 100 for heavy vehicles and ₹ 30 from cars and jeeps will be levied by the Mussoorie Municipal Board either through its employees or contracted agents at Kolhukhet - Mussoorie's entry point.

The Shimla Municipal Corporation has decided to impose green tax on vehicles bearing registration numbers of other states.

In Goa, massive pollution, emission and discharge of effluents were leaving carbon footprints on State's environment. In order to overcome this problem, the Goa Government in 2013 has introduced Goa Cess on Products and Substances Causing Pollution (Green Cess) Act, the state government has also opened the way to the Environment and Energy Audit Bureau (EAEB) to identify sensitive areas of energy and environment conservation. The act, imposes a tax "not exceeding two per cent" on all products which leave behind a carbon footprint due to "handling, consumption, utilisation, transportation, combustion or movement causing pollution of lithosphere, atmosphere, biosphere, hydrosphere and other environmental resources". The cess will also be imposed on all products which "cause emission of carbon dioxide and other greenhouse gases or discharge of other types of effluents, including asphalts, lubricants, naptha, waxes and other hydrocarbon compounds". The new law also brings in its ambit other polluting industries like mining, transportation and iron ore processing.

In 2012, a study funded by the UK's Foreign and Commonwealth Office has suggested adoption of fiscal incentives by the State Governments can pave the way for environment-friendly industrial development. The study has recommended a slew of fiscal instruments that Tamil Nadu, West Bengal and Odisha can use to reduce carbon emissions while promoting industrial growth. For West Bengal and Odisha, the study suggests measures such as low carbon refunding schemes for power sector, industry and waste management, where environment-friendly projects such as renewable energy are supported by conventional industry; grants and funds; incentives for renewable energy, including waste heat recovery and for green buildings. In Tamil Nadu, the study suggests a green cess on conventional power generation and power consumers that could be used to fund renewable energy projects support to cement industries to set up equipment in their kilns to burn, tax incentives for green buildings and to the transportation sector to encourage alternative fuels.

Conclusion

Pollution in India has emerged as a serious problem which has huge implication for sustainability of growth due to rapid depletion of natural resources. Among these two approaches, regulatory (or "command-and-control") and use of market-based instruments (such as taxes and tradable permits), the latter has certain edge. The two approaches are certainly not mutually exclusive and can be used in judicious combination of each other. In developed countries, mainly western European nations, Canada, New Zealand, Australia, etc. there has been shift towards market based approach to solve environmental problems and India needs to move towards adopting market-based instruments to solve its environmental problems which has reached at alarming level.

Annex

F.No.354/72/2010-TRU
Government of India
Ministry of Finance
Department of Revenue
(Tax Research Unit)

New Delhi, dated the 24th June, 2010.

To

Chief Commissioners of Central Excise (All),

Chief Commissioners of Customs (All),

Chief Commissioners of Central Excise and Customs (All),

Director General of Central Excise Intelligence, New Delhi,

Director General of Audit, N. Delhi,

Director General of Revenue Intelligence, New Delhi.

Madam/Sir,

Subject: Levy of Clean Energy Cess - regarding.

It may kindly be recalled that as part of the proposals

contained in the Budget for 2010-11, Finance Minister had announced the imposition of Clean Energy Cess as a duty of excise on coal, lignite and peat. This cess is to come into force on a date to be notified by the Central Government after the enactment of the Finance Bill, 2010. In pursuance of the enactment of the Bill on 08.05.2010, it has been decided **to notify 1st July, 2010 as the appointed date** for coming into force of the provisions of Chapter VII (Section 83 and 84) of the Finance Act, 2010. Notification No. 1/2010-CEC (Clean Energy Cess) dated 22.06.2010 has been issued for this purpose.

2. The Tenth Schedule to the Finance Act, 2010 prescribes a statutory rate of cess of Rs.100 per tonne for all three categories, namely, coal, lignite and peat. An effective rate of Rs.50 per tonne has been prescribed through Notification No. 3/2010-CEC dated 22.06.2010. Notification No. 28/2010-CE and 29/2010-CE, both dated 22.06.2010 have also been issued to exempt such goods (i.e to which the clean energy cess applies) from education cess and higher education cess respectively. As a result the aggregate rate of cess would be Rs.50 per tonne. This amount has to be paid in cash as suitable amendment in the CENVAT credit rules ,2004 is being made to exclude payment of this cess using credit.

3. The cess would apply to the gross quantity of raw coal, lignite or peat raised and dispatched from a coal mine. No deduction from this quantity is to be allowed for loss, if any, on account of washing of coal or its conversion into any other product/form prior to its dispatch from the mine. At the same time, cess would not be chargeable on washed coal or any other form provided the appropriate cess has been paid at the raw stage. In order to provide for this, all goods covered by the Tenth Schedule other than raw coal, raw lignite and peat are being exempted from the cess (Notification No. 4/2010-CEC dated 22.06.2010) on the condition that appropriate cess has been paid at the raw stage.

4. Since Clean Energy Cess is being levied as a duty of excise, it would also apply to imported coal by virtue of Section 3(1) of the Customs Tariff Act in the form of additional duty of customs. As imported coal would not satisfy the condition regarding payment of appropriate cess at the raw stage, Clean Energy Cess would apply to all forms of imported coal including washed coal.

5. In the State of Meghalaya, coal is mined under traditional and customary rights vested on the local tribes. The mines operated by these tribes are not subjected to the provisions of laws that regulate the operation of coal mines. As such, full exemption from Clean Energy Cess is being provided to coal produced in the State of Meghalaya under such rights (Notification No. 5/2010-CEC dated 22.06.2010 refers).

6. Section 83 of the Finance Act, 2010 provides that the Central Government may by notification in the official gazette declare that any of the provisions of Central Excise Act, 1944 relating to levy, exemption, refund etc. would be applicable in respect of Clean energy Cess. In pursuance of this power, Notification No. 2/2010-Clean Energy Cess dated 22.06.2010 has been issued to borrow the relevant machinery provisions of the Central Excise Act, 1944 for the collection and administration of the cess.

7. Section 84 of the Finance Act, 2010 empowers the Central Government to make rules for carrying out the provisions of Chapter VII. Accordingly, Clean Energy Cess Rules, 2010 have been notified under this provision to prescribe a procedure for the levy and collection of the cess (Notification No. 6/2010- Clean Energy Cess dated 22.06.2010). These rules envisage simple compliance regime for coal mines akin to the one already in place in respect of stowing Excise Duty collected by the office of the Coal Controller, Government of India. The salient features of these rules are as under:

(i) Every producer of coal, lignite and peat is required to be registered with the jurisdictional central excise authority.

This would imply that every coal mine should obtain registration. In several cases, especially in the case of coal mines operated by public sector undertakings such as Coal India Limited and its subsidiaries, the accounting and billing of coal is done in a centralised manner. In order to ease the compliance burden on such producers, an option has been given to obtain centralised registration for the office from where accounting or billing is done. With the introduction of ACES, the registration of Central Excise assessees is being undertaken exclusively in the electronic mode. Besides, the registration number generated electronically is required for making electronic payments of duty. In order to harmonise the processes in respect of Clean Energy Cess with Central Excise it has been decided that the application form for registration of Central Excise assessees would itself be used for the registration of assessees liable to pay Clean Energy Cess with the modification that the word "factory" would be read as "mine" in this case.

(ii) Cess would be payable on quantity removed during a month on self assessment basis.

(iii) The due date for payment has been fixed as the 6th (for e- payment) / 5th (for payment in any other manner) of the month following the next month to which the removals relate i.e. payment for removals during the month of July,2010 should be paid by the 5th/6th of September,2010. However, on imports the cess would be payable w.e.f. 1st July, 2010.

(iv) Adjustment of excess payment, if any, is permissible by the next payment date.

(v) Monthly return indicating the total quantity removed along with cess payment has been prescribed. Since this return is not compatible with ACES software electronic filing would not be feasible at this stage. Returns may hence be accepted manually by the jurisdictional Range/Division of Central Excise.

(vi) General penalty of Rs 10,000 has been prescribed for any contravention.

(vii) Specified goods are to be removed under cover of proper documents. However, this need not be an invoice. It has been prescribed in rule that any document specifying the quantity removed and name of the consignee would suffice.

8. Although the levy of Clean Energy Cess comes into force on the 1st of July, 2010, the first payment from registered producers would be due only by the 5th of September, 2010. In the meanwhile, the office of Chief Controller of Accounts has already been requested to assign a minor head for the payment of this cess both on domestic and imported coal. Relevant communication conveying this to the field formations would be issued in due course.

9. The provisions of the relevant notifications and this letter may be brought to the notice of field formations under your charge and the trade. The notifications may kindly be studied with utmost care and difficulties in their implementation, if any, may be brought to the notice of the undersigned.

Yours Faithfully,

(Vivek Johri)

Joint Secretary (TRU-I)

Tel: 23092687

Bibliography

"Baumal, W.J and W.E. Oates (1987), The Theory of Environmental Policy, 2nd edition, Cambridge, Cambridge University Press.

CMIE (2001), Industry: Market Size and Shares, Centre for Monitoring Indian Economy, Mumbai, India.

CMIE (2002), Industry: Market Size and Shares, Centre for Monitoring Indian Economy, Mumbai, India.

Coase, R.H. (1960); "The Problem of Social Cost", Journal of Law and Economics, 3:1-44, University of Chicago.

CPCB (2000); "Clean Coal Initiatives", Parivesh Newsletter, Central Pollution Control Board, New Delhi.

Divan, S. And A. Rosencranz (2001), Environmental Law and Policy in India, Oxford University Press, New Delhi.

Government of India (Ministry of Environment and Forests) (1992). Policy Statement for Abatement of Pollution, New Delhi.

Government of India (Ministry of Finance) (1992). Report of the Tax Reforms Committee, An Interim Report (Chaired by Raja J. Chelliah), New Delhi.

Government of India; (Planning Commission), Ninth Five Year Plan, New Delhi.

Government of India; (Ministry of Environment and Forests) (2001); Battery (Management and Handing) Rules.

Government of India; (2002); Expert Committee Report on Auto Fuel Policy.

Mehta, S., S. Mundle and U. Sankar (1993/1997); Controlling Pollution: Incentives and Regulation, Sage Publications, New Delhi.

Mukherjee, S. and S. Sud (2003); A Comparative Study of the Impact of Emissions from Diesel and Petrol Fuelled Passenger Cars; A Joint Study of Madras School of Economics and Delphi-TVS Diesel Systems Ltd.

National Institute of Public Finance and Policy (1997); Report of the Task, Force to Evaluate Market-based Instruments for Industrial Pollution Abatement, National Institute of Public Finance and Policy, New Delhi.

National Plastic Waste Management Task Force Report (1997); Accessed from http://www.netpem.org/announcement/workshops/plastic/IndianPlastic ManagementScenario.pdf.

O'Conner, D. (1998); "Applying Economic Instruments in Developing Countries: From Theory to Implementation"; Environment and Developing Economics, Vol 4.

Organisation for Economic Co-operation and Development (OECD) (1992); Economic Instruments for Environmental Management in Developing Countries, Paris.

OECD (1994); Managing the Environment: The Role of Economic Instruments, Paris.

OECD (1995). Environmental Funds in Economies in Transition, Paris.

OECD Papers: (1996, 1997) OECD, Paris (www.oecd.org).

OECD (2001); Environmentally Related Taxes in OECD Countries-Issues and Strategies, OECD, Paris.

OECD (2002); Environmentally Related Taxes in OECD Countries-Issues and Strategies, Paris.

Pigou, A.C. (1920); Economics of Welfare, Macmillan, London.

Sankar, U. (2002); "On the Design and Environment of Fiscal Instruments for Pollution Control in India", M. Govinda Rao (ed.), Development, Poverty and Public Policy, Oxford University Press.

Sankar, U. and O.P. Mathur (1998); Economic Instruments for Environment Sustainability; National Institute of Public Finance and Policy and Madras School of Economics.

Tietenberg, T.H. (1985); Marketable Emission Permits: Reforming Pollution Policy, Resources for the Future, Washington DC.

Karpagam M; (1999); Environmental policy; Sterling Publishers Pvt. Ltd.

United Nations, Conference on Environment and Development, (1992). Agenda 21, Rio de Janeiro.

World Bank (1997), "A Planner's Guide for Selecting Clean-Coal Technologies for Power Plants", World Bank Paper No. 387, Washington DC, USA.

World Bank. (2000), Greening Industry, New Roles for Communities, Markets and Governments, Oxford University Press, New York.

World Bank, Ministry of Environment and Forests and Confederation of Indian Industry (2002). International Workshop on Economic Instruments for Industrial Pollution Prevention and Control in India, Proceedings, New Delhi.

World Commission for Environment and Development (1987); Our Common Future, Oxford University Press, New York.

Agnieszka Laskowska and Frank Scrimgeour; Environmental Taxation: The European Experience.

Environmental Taxes: (Nov 2000); Recent development in tools for integration, European Environment Agency.

Draft paper on Eco taxes of Ministry of Environment, Forest and Climate Change.

UK Round Table on Sustainable Development; (2000); Not too difficult- Economic instruments to provide sustainable development within a modernized Economy, London

UK Government (1999); Budget (1999) London.

UK Department for the Environment, Transport and the Regions (DETR), The Environmental Appraisal of the Fuel Duly Escalator, Memorandum, London.

Swedish Environmental Protection Agency, Environmental Taxes in Sweden, Stockholm.

SEO (1998) Research of the Impact of the Regulatory Energy Tax in Business Firms, University Amsterdam.

Togeby, Mikael; (1998); Evaluation of the Danish taxes and agreements, Copenhagen.

Ministry of Environment and Forests, (2006), National Environment Policy (NEP).

Ministry of Environment and Forests, (1986), The Environment (Protection) Act.

Ministry of Environment and Forests, (1974), The Water (Prevention and Control of Pollution) Act.

Ministry of Environment and Forests, (1977), The Water (Prevention and Control of Pollution) Cess Act.

Ministry of Environment and Forests, (1981), The Air (Prevention & Control Of Pollution) Act.

Ministry of Environment and Forests, (2010), The National Green Tribunal (NGT) Act.

Ministry of Environment and Forests, (2009), State of Environment(SoE) Report - India.

Ministry of Environment and Forests, (2013-14), Annual Report.

Ministry of Environment and Forests, (2012-13), Report to the People.

https:// www.powermin.nic.in

https:// www.mnre.gov.in

https:// www.cpcb.nic.in

https:// www.commerce.nic.in

https:// www.bis.org.in

https:// www.beeindia.in